BEGINNER'S GUIDE TO SELLING ON EBAY

How To Start & Grow a Successful Online Reselling Business from Home

2022 Edition

By Ann Eckhart

TABLE OF CONTENTS

INTRODUCTION

CHAPTER ONE: THE BASICS OF EBAY

CHAPTER TWO: EBAY FEES & FEATURES

CHAPTER THREE: RESELLING EQUIPMENT & SUPPLIES

CHAPTER FOUR: WHAT TO SELL & WHERE TO SOURCE

CHAPTER FIVE: RESELLING CLOTHING

CHAPTER SIX: TAKING EBAY PHOTOS

CHAPTER SEVEN: CREATING EBAY LISTINGS

CHAPTER EIGHT: EBAY SHIPPING MADE EASY

CHAPTER NINE: PROCESSING ORDERS

CHAPTER TEN: MARKETING & PROMOTION

CHAPTER ELEVEN: MANAGING AN EBAY STORE

CHAPTER TWELVE: TAKING EBAY TO THE NEXT LEVEL

CHAPTER THIRTEEN: EBAY ACCOUNTING MADE EASY

CHAPTER FOURTEEN: CUSTOMER SERVICE

CONCLUSION

ABOUT THE AUTHOR

INTRODUCTION

Welcome to the Beginner's Guide to Selling on Ebay: 2022 Edition! My name is Ann Eckhart, and I have been reselling on Ebay since 2005. I have also been educating others about selling on the platform for nearly as long through YouTube videos and books, as well as in hundreds of posts on social media sites such as Facebook, Twitter, Instagram, Pinterest, and TikTok.

However, out of all the Ebay content I have produced over the years, this book is by far the most popular because it teaches people EXACTLY how to source, list, and ship items on Ebay. I release a new, updated version of this book every year, and it continues to outsell all my other books combined.

And new for 2022 is that I have combined and updated all the information that was in a second book, *Ebay Seller Secrets*, into THIS book so that you can not only learn how to start selling on Ebay but also how to take your business to the next level. While the title of this book remains *Beginner's Guide to Selling on Ebay*, it is the ULTIMATE GUIDE to Ebay!

So why would anyone need to read a book about selling on Ebay? Isn't that information available for free online? Well, sort of. Sure, there are active reselling communities on Facebook, Instagram, and YouTube where people post all sorts of information.

However, what you likely find online are only the best parts of selling on Ebay. The huge hauls, the giant package piles, the impressive gross sales numbers.

But those post only give you a glimpse into the world of Ebay. They do not give you the whole picture. They are not always honest about the time and effort required to source items to resell. They do not share how many hours were spent packaging up low-dollar orders. And they do not share the actual net profit after all fees and taxes are taken out.

This book, however, tells you the TRUTH about selling on Ebay, the good and the bad, so that you have all the information necessary to make your Ebay journey a success. After all, I am assuming that you want to sell on Ebay to MAKE MONEY....and that is what this book will help you do.

Ebay can be a lot of fun, and there is good money to be made on the site. But there are right ways to do things and wrong ways to do things. This book will cover everything you need to know to sell on Ebay the right way, from how to successfully find items to resell and how to list them to how to handle customer service issues and track your financials.

And, sure, while it is easy to tell people just to log on to Ebay.com and follow the on-screen instructions to learn how to list items for sale, those who have no experience with the Ebay website often want someone to walk them through the entire process. And that is what I will be doing in this book, walking you step-by-step through everything you need to do to get started selling on Ebay. Plus, I will also be sharing all the insider tips and tricks that the Ebay website does not tell you.

This book is for both beginners and for those who are already selling online and those who want to take their Ebay business to the next level. I will be going over the basics of selling on Ebay, walking you through setting up your account, finding profitable items to sell, taking photographs, creating your first listings, figuring out shipping, and packaging up orders. I will also share tips and tricks for dealing with problems, communicating with customers, and managing your Ebay accounting.

But I will also help you grow your Ebay business from a hobby level to a part-time or even full-time business. While you may not want to scale up to a sizeable reselling business, after reading this book, you will at least have the information you need if you decide you want to do so in the future.

Ebay is a unique marketplace with its own unique learning curve to master. However, after reading this book, you will be able to jump into selling on Ebay and earning money right off the bat. And if you have already been selling on the site, hopefully I have given you some information to help you grow your business.

I know that Ebay can seem overwhelming at first (even I was scared to use it before I started my business), but once you have a few listings under your belt and have shipped out a couple of orders, you will realize how easy it is. And if you are like me, you will wonder why it took you so long to give Ebay a try!

CHAPTER ONE:

THE BASICS OF EBAY

Ebay debuted in 1995 as an online classified ads marketplace, one of the first online shopping websites. It offered people all over America the ability to list items they had for sale and sell them to customers in every state.

When Ebay first started, it was an online auction site; people put their items up for auction, and customers bid on them. The highest bidder won the item, paid the seller through Ebay's payment system, PayPal, and then the seller shipped the winning bidder their merchandise. In the beginning, customers could also bypass PayPal altogether and mail checks to sellers, and sometimes they even sent cash. Yes, you read that right: people mailed strangers envelopes filled with cash to pay for their Ebay items!

After initially being only available in the United States, Ebay quickly expanded to both sellers and buyers worldwide. While auctions and antiques remain what the site is known for, these days, sellers large and small can also sell both new and used products through Ebay at what is called **Fixed Price**. When listing an item at Fixed Price, the seller sets the price, also called a **Buy It Now** price, and there is no auction, no bidding. Today, most items that sell on the site are sold at Fixed Price, although the auction option still exists.

I sometimes miss the days when you could start every item at a 99-cent auction and watch the bidding go up and up. I remember sitting at my desk and hitting the refresh button on my computer every minute to update the bidding, watching the price rise until the auction ended. However, those days are long gone except for scarce, in-demand collectibles. Nowadays, Ebay is mainly a buy-it-now shopping site, just like Amazon, Walmart, and other retailers. And while nostalgia for "the old days" remains, Ebay now functions much like every other shopping website, giving it an even playing field.

One thing that was always unique to Ebay was **PayPal**, which was Ebay's payment processing system. For buyers to shop on Ebay, they used to have a PayPal account. PayPal allowed buyers to set up multiple funding sources, everything from their bank accounts and their own PayPal balances to their debit and credit cards, to pay for items on Ebay. Sellers also had to have a PayPal account to facilitate their orders and to get paid. PayPal was the payment system that everyone on Ebay, regardless of whether they were buying or selling, HAD to use.

However, in 2015, Ebay and PayPal split, becoming two individual companies with no ties to one another. And while Ebay continued to rely on PayPal as their payment processor for several years, in 2019, Ebay introduced its own payment system, called **Managed Payments.**

As of this writing, most Ebay sellers are now enrolled in Ebay's Managed Payments. Managed Payments is Ebay's very own payment processing system; it works just like PayPal did, but it does not require the extra step of needing to have a PayPal account. Now, Managed Payments allows customers to purchase items directly on the Ebay site without being directed to use their PayPal accounts.

In short, buyers can now shop on Ebay the same way they do on most other websites. And just like PayPal, buyers can pay via Managed Payments using various methods, including credit cards, debit cards, bank accounts, and even PayPal. I still use PayPal to pay for my own Ebay purchases, although it is connected to one of my credit cards as I no longer have a running PayPal balance from my Ebay sales.

For Ebay sellers, Managed Payments means that Ebay, not PayPal, now manages their funds. When someone purchases one of your items on Ebay, Ebay will process their payment, deduct the fees and shipping costs (after you have printed off the shipping label) associated with the transaction, and then disperse the remaining funds to you. You can choose to have your funds dispersed daily or weekly. Don't worry: we will tackle the payment process in-depth later in this book.

I have been selling on Ebay since 2005, and I have shipped items to every corner of the globe. When I first started selling on Ebay, it was one of the few online shopping sites on the internet, meaning you could sell nearly anything on it. In fact, when I started to sell online, Ebay and Amazon were pretty much the only two e-commerce sites available to sell or buy on.

Today, however, Ebay competes with not only Amazon but also Walmart for the top marketplace spot. Plus, nearly every retailer, both large and small, has its own website. And sites like Poshmark, Etsy, Mercari, and even Facebook Marketplace are only making the online reselling landscape even more crowded.

The competition between online sellers is much fiercer than when I first started selling online, too. Therefore, the types of items that sell and the methods in which they sell have also significantly changed. Many sellers now turn to Amazon to sell their new goods, while Ebay is more centered on secondhand items.

However, while things may not always sell as fast as they once did on Ebay, you can still sell almost anything there, new or used. And, more and more companies are expanding onto Ebay to sell their goods the same way they sell them on their own websites as well as through other retailers.

Plus, with shoppers no longer needing a PayPal account to shop on Ebay, the site is much more user-friendly and accessible. Today the sky's the limit for what you can sell on Ebay, whether new or used, and the customers are just as diverse as the offerings.

Despite the competition, Ebay is still the number one site for individuals and small businesses to sell their items to people worldwide. While it is much larger than it was initially, at its core, Ebay still functions like the world's largest flea market with items of every type and at every price point available. Ebay continues to expand and improve, giving sellers like me confidence that they will be around for years to come. With nearly two hundred million registered Ebay users, there are still plenty of opportunities to make money on Ebay.

But why sell your items on Ebay as opposed to a garage sale or consignment shop? Hands down, you will get the most money for your items on Ebay versus selling them locally. As I mentioned earlier, there are nearly 200 million registered Ebay users, meaning there are 200 million more chances to sell your items.

Let's say you have a rare collectible to sell. While only a handful of people will come to your garage sale or enter your local consignment shop, on Ebay, your item is available for purchase to the millions of Ebay account holders around the world. You only need to wait for that one buyer to find your item for you to get top dollar for it. The chances of that same buyer coming to your garage sale are slim to none, but the odds are much better the customer will find you on Ebay.

Plus, learning to sell on Ebay provides you with a certain financial protection level. Once you know how to sell on Ebay, you can sell your unwanted items for top dollar at any time, raising cash quickly if the need arises. While you could maybe earn a couple of hundred dollars fast by selling your stuff at a garage sale, you can rake in a few thousand dollars for those same items after a couple of weeks of them being listed on Ebay!

Most people who sell on Ebay got their start by selling their unwanted possessions from their own homes. And once they were hooked on selling off their own stuff, they started searching thrift stores and garage sales for more items to flip, which makes Ebay the perfect place for both hobby and full-time sellers.

If you are already selling on Ebay, you have both an Ebay account and likely a PayPal account. You may have also already opted into Ebay's new Managed Payments program. However, if you are new to Ebay, there are some initial steps you need to take before you can list anything for sale.

How To Set Up Your Ebay Account: Signing up for an Ebay account is the first step toward selling on Ebay. Ebay makes this process very easy; simply visit **Ebay.com** and click on **Register** in the top left corner of the page to get started.

When signing up for an Ebay account, you will first need to select a **User Name**, also referred to as a *screen name.* Think carefully about the name you choose; you do not want to give out too much information (such as *singlewomanlivingalone*), but you also do not want to have a crazy name no one understands (what does *dhioatg89yrew* mean, anyway?). Selecting an easy-to-remember user name will help you attract repeat customers and build your brand.

Since there are millions of registered Ebay users, chances are the first name you want to use may already be taken, so have a few options ready. If you think you might want to sell on Ebay consistently in the future, choose a name that reflects what you plan to sell.

Next, you will need to provide your **Social Security number** and **financial information** to create your Ebay account, either a **bank account routing number** or a **credit card**.

You need to provide your Social Security number for tax purposes. If you **sell more than $600 a year on Ebay**, they will provide you with a **1099 tax form** in January to file with the IRS. When PayPal issued the tax forms, the threshold was $20,000; but the new $600 threshold aligns with what most other companies use when issuing 1099 forms. Don't worry: Ebay will notify you when you have a tax form available.

After providing your Social Security number, you will also need to enter your **banking information** to register for **Managed Payments**, which is how buyers will pay for the items they buy from you and how Ebay will distribute your earnings. It is also essential, I believe, to have a **credit card** on file with Ebay as a backup funding source.

Note that while Ebay will deduct your fees and shipping charges from your pending balance, it is still a good idea to have a credit card on file just in case there is a charge that your balance or bank account does not cover. I do not want a billing dispute to disrupt my sales, and I do not want Ebay to withdraw money from my checking account that may be delegated to something else, so a credit card on file gives me an added layer of protection.

As I have already discussed, in 2015, Ebay and PayPal split into two separate companies, with Ebay implementing their own payment system called **Managed Payments.** By the time of this book's publication, all Ebay sellers should already be enrolled in Managed Payments. If you are just now setting up your Ebay account, you will be enrolled in Managed Payments right from the start.

When Ebay sellers used PayPal, we were billed for our monthly fees, which we had to manually pay, either from our PayPal balances, credits cards, or checking accounts. The great thing about Ebay's Managed Payments is that Ebay now takes out all listing fees, postage costs, and store subscription fees once a transaction is completed. That means the only money left in your account will all be dispersed to you; you no longer have a monthly invoice of fees to pay, which was what sellers had to do when PayPal processed all payments.

Once you have your Ebay account set up and are enrolled in Managed Payments, it is time to experiment with the Ebay site itself. I believe there are three steps you should take to learn precisely how Ebay works:

Step #1: Buy Some Low-Dollar Items: After you have set up your Ebay and Managed Payments accounts, purchase some cheap items from several different Ebay sellers (there are millions of no-risk 99-cent items on the site) to familiarize yourself with not only Ebay's search feature but also the checkout process.

This is not the time to try to get a deal on an expensive electronic; you want to simply go through the Ebay buying process so that you will see things the way your potential customers will once you have items listed for sale. By buying a handful of items, you will see how different sellers treat their customers and how they ship their merchandise.

Look at how other sellers write their listings. Were their titles and descriptions accurate? Study the photos they provide. Are the pictures clear and well-lit? Note how you receive notification of payment and shipment, and keep track of how long it takes your order to arrive. Carefully examine how the item was packaged. Was your order shipped quickly and in clean packaging? Were breakables well protected? Did the seller leave you feedback?

Everything you learn as a buyer will translate to how you function as a seller. Note the things you liked and did not like about the orders you received and use that knowledge to create your own listings. It is the Golden Rule of business: Treat your customers as you would want to be treated.

Step #2: Sell Some of Your Personal Items: After you are comfortable *buying* on Ebay, it is time to get your feet wet *selling* by listing some items from around your own home. Do not worry about sourcing products until you are comfortable with the selling process.

Again, as you learned about what other sellers do when you bought from them, selling some of your own items allows you to experience being a seller yourself without the risk of spending money on inventory.

Selling some of the items you already own (books, CDs, video games, clothing, toys, collectibles) will give you experience in writing titles and descriptions, taking photos, and preparing shipments. Again, these initial sales are not about making much money; the goal is to gain experience as a seller, both in how the Ebay site works and how to ship out items.

You may not even make any money from these sales; heck, you might even lose a few dollars. But the experience you will gain will be invaluable as you continue your Ebay journey.

Experiment with the first items you list. Try 99-cent auctions. Try listing *Fixed Price* both with *Best Offer* and without. Try both calculated, flat rate, and free shipping. Try sending *Offers to Watchers*. Ebay offers so many ways to sell; you want to familiarize yourself with all of them so that you will know which ones to use going forward.

By playing around with all the various ways available for you to sell items on Ebay, you will find the methods that you are most comfortable with. You may decide to offer "free shipping" on small, lightweight objects ("free" is in quotes as shipping is never free; someone, in this case, you as the seller, will have to pay for it) while using calculated shipping on larger, heavier things. You may decide that auctions do not work for what you are selling and choose just to list items at a fixed price. You may decide that you enjoy the haggling of offering "best offer," or you may, like me, find out that you hate dealing with offers and not add it as an option to your listings. You may try accepting returns athen turn them off later down the road.

As you experiment with the various ways to sell, remember that you are not locked into any one listing method. After nearly two decades of selling on Ebay, I still frequently change things up. What makes Ebay so unique is that each seller gets to decide for themselves how they want to sell their items. The individual control we have as sellers is what sets Ebay apart from the other reselling sites.

Step #3: Source a Small Number of Items to Sell: By now, you have set up your Ebay and Managed Payments accounts, you have purchased a handful of low-dollar items, and you have sold some things from around your house. Now it is time to get serious and source some items from outside of your home to resell!

While it is tempting to head to the nearest garage sale and buy everything they have, do not invest much money in products to resell right away. Start small with some thrift store or yard sale finds, or try your hand at reselling new items you see on clearance at retail stores.

Again, these first few items you buy to flip do not have to be big moneymakers. You are still gaining experience as a seller before you jump into making Ebay an actual job. I recommend giving yourself a budget, say $20, the first time you go sourcing. See how far $20 gets you at your local thrift store or at neighborhood garage sales. Do not let yourself source anything else until you list what you already bought.

The first few times I went to estate sales to find items to resell were a disaster. I bought things that ended up being worthless. However, since I stuck to a strict budget, I did not berate myself for wasting my money. Instead, I considered these first purchases part of "buying my education." The next time I went sourcing, I did a little better. And then next time, better than that. It takes time to recognize what is worth picking up and what you should just leave behind. We will go over what sells best on Ebay later in this book.

Why Take It Slow: Why don't I recommend you jump into selling on Ebay with both feet and see what happens? Well, first off, Ebay is a unique marketplace. You can buy and sell at auction or fixed price. You can accept offers and send offers to interested customers. To sell on Ebay, you need to source products, take and edit photos, write up listings, handle customer questions, and ship out packages. You may find that after buying and selling a few things that you do not even like selling on Ebay, and you may decide not to pursue it as a job or even as a hobby.

However, if you find that you enjoy selling on Ebay, going through these first steps will give you a good base of knowledge before starting a full-fledged business, whether part-time or full-time. Plus, you will gain some feedback, which is very important in earning potential customers' trust. The more positive feedback you have, the more customers will trust you, and the more benefits you will gain from Ebay, such as *Top-Rated Seller* rankings and discounts on fees.

Also, because of the limits Ebay now places on new sellers, if you are entirely new to the site, you will be forced to take it slow regardless of how many items you want to list. Ebay is constantly changing what they require of new sellers. After creating an account, Ebay will walk you through their current selling and buying limits and requirements, including exactly how many listings they will give you to start with.

If you start off selling strong, you can contact Ebay directly to ask them to increase your listing allotment. You will need to prove that you are following Ebay's policies and providing the best customer service possible for them to grant you more listings.

I see so many new Ebay sellers dive headfirst into trying to make Ebay their full-time business, and many of them fail miserably. Ebay has a steep learning curve. Take your time to learn Ebay's systems and policies so that when you do start to list a lot of items with the goal of earning real money, you will be successful!

CHAPTER TWO:

EBAY FEES & FEATURES

Ebay and the Ebay interface have evolved over the years, and they are constantly rolling out new features to help us as sellers. In this chapter, I will be going over all Ebay's fees and the features you can use to manage what you are selling.

Selling Fees: Ebay is sometimes jokingly referred to as *FeeBay* because of the fees associated with selling on the site. There are three different types of fees you must pay when you sell on Ebay:

1. **Insertion Fees:** As of this writing, Ebay is currently giving all sellers up to 250 zero insertion fees every month. Those with an Ebay Store are given more depending on their store subscription level, which we'll talk more about later in this book. After you have used up your zero-insertion fee allowance, your insertion fees will be charged per listing based on the category you are selling in. Most items incur a 35-cent insertion fee, although it varies by category. Ebay is also constantly offering special promotions on insertion fees, and, as I mentioned, fees can be lower if you have an Ebay Store subscription.
2. **Final Value Fees:** Ebay charges you a *Final Value Fee* when your items sell. The fee is calculated as a per-

centage of the total amount of the sale, including any shipping charges. Final Value Fees are anywhere from 2% up to 15%, depending on the item's category and whether you have a Store subscription.
3. **Ebay Store Subscription Fees:** A great way to save on fees and organize your Ebay listings is to open an Ebay Store. An Ebay Store is an optional feature that you pay extra for; it is unnecessary to have a store to sell on Ebay. As of this writing, Ebay offers five different store subscription levels. We will go over the store options later in this book.

Ebay Listing Variations: As you play around with buying and selling on Ebay, you will start to become familiar with the various methods available for listings, including:

- **Auctions:** Auction listings feature items that potential buyers place bids on. Say you find an item you like that is listed at auction for 99-cents. You simply put in the minimum bid increment to place a bid, which varies depending on the current bid. Sellers can choose to run auctions for one, three, five, seven, or ten days. Note that seven-day auctions are the most popular as they give potential buyers a whole week to find the item and place their bids.
- **Auctions with Buy It Now:** Ebay sellers have the option to add a Buy It Now feature to their auctions, which not only offers customers the chance to bid on an item but also provides buyers the ability to buy the item outright without bidding. For instance, you may see an auction with a starting bid of 99-cents but also with a Buy It Now option of $10. Buyers can either bid on that listing or buy the item outright. Once the first bid is placed, the Buy It Now option disappears.
- **Fixed Price:** Ebay began as an online auction site, but today most listings are Fixed Price with Buy It Now as

the only option available to customers. Fixed Price listings only offer the option of purchasing the item outright; there is no option to bid.
- **Fixed Price with Best Offer:** Many Ebay sellers turn the Best Offer feature on in their listings, stating a set Fixed Price but with the option for buyers to submit Best Offers for consideration. Let's say you see an item listed for $50 with the Best Offer option. You submit an offer to the seller for, say, $40. If the seller accepts, you are then required to purchase the item for $40. However, the seller could counteroffer, let's say, coming back with a price of $45. You could accept the counteroffer, or you could make another counteroffer of your own. Or the seller could simply reject your offer outright. Most sellers accept reasonable offers. You can even select a minimum threshold amount for Ebay to automatically accept on your behalf. Going back to that $ 50 item, let's say the seller turned on the auto-accept feature to accept any offer of $40 or more. So, if you offered them $40, your offer would be automatically accepted; you would not have to wait for the seller to accept your offer manually.
- **Offers To Watchers:** Starting in 2019, Ebay gave sellers the ability to send offers to interested buyers. When at least one person "watches" an item you have listed, you can send them a direct offer of either a percentage or a dollar amount off. The offer you send is good for up to 48 hours. Note that you will not see the user name of the person you are sending the offer to. Ebay does not show sellers the watchers' names, just the number of watchers on any single item.

Feedback: Once you have purchased some items on Ebay, you will want to follow through with leaving **Feedback**. A unique feature of Ebay is its feedback system, where both buyers and sellers can leave each other feedback on transactions. Buyers can leave sellers *Positive*, Neutral, or Negative feedback; sellers can only leave buyers Positive feedback.

In addition to the Feedback rating, buyers and sellers can also leave comments. Buyers can also rate their experience using a five-star system on the following factors:

- Item as Described
- Communication
- Shipping Time
- Shipping & Handling Charges

Good feedback is key to having a successful selling career on Ebay. Getting negative feedback will seriously lower your overall feedback rating. A buyer who "dings" your stars (i.e., leaves you lower than the ideal five-stars) hurts your seller rating. And your seller rating directly impacts any potential fee or shipping discounts you may be eligible for.

A solid feedback score and seller rating not only make potential customers more likely to buy from you, but they are also crucial in maintaining your Ebay account. Ebay has cracked down in recent years, suspending accounts and kicking bad sellers off their site. You want to do everything you can to make sure your buyers are happy and that they do not leave you negative feedback or low star ratings.

As a buyer, you want to leave honest but fair feedback. If you receive the item you ordered when the seller promised, and it is in the condition it was advertised as there is no need to leave the seller anything other than positive feedback with five-stars. Sellers typically block buyers who consistently leave negative feedback for most of their purchases (yes, not only can buyers view your feedback, but you can see theirs). When it comes to feedback, I take the Golden Rule approach in that I leave the feedback for others that I would want them to leave me!

Seller Hub: As an Ebay seller, you will be spending a lot of your time on the *Seller Hub* page of your Ebay account. In fact, this is the page that I have bookmarked on my computer as it is the starting point for almost everything I need to access while using Ebay.

The *Seller Hub* has seven tabs at the top of the page; there are additional options under most of these:

- Overview
- Orders
- Listings
- Marketing
- Performance
- Payments
- Research

Overview: The *Overview* page is the default page for *Seller Hub*. Here you are given a quick look at your current Ebay statistics, including:

- Unread Messages
- Orders Awaiting Shipment
- Sales for the Past 31 Days
- Seller Level
- Today's Feedback
- Growth Recommendation

There are then several sections of data that you can really dig into as you scroll further along the page, including:

Tasks: Here, you will see everything Ebay needs you to act on, including answering messages or shipping orders. They also offer *Suggested Actions* for things like updating listings and sending offers to watchers.

Sales: Ebay shows you your sales from the current day as well as the *Last seven days, Last 31 days,* and *Last 90 days.*

Orders: Ebay breaks down your order history here, everything from the number of orders you need to ship and those awaiting payment to how many orders are awaiting your feedback and if you are eligible for any unpaid item cases. You can click through to any of these options to complete the tasks.

Listings: This section shows you all your listing information, everything from your total number of active listings to unsold listings. You can click through to any line item to be taken directly to that data.

Sales (last 31 days): Ebay shows you your sales compared to the previous month and the same period a year ago. You can adjust the dates to narrow down your sales numbers further.

Traffic: Real-time traffic to your listings.

Seller Level: Here, you can track your current seller level and the statistics Ebay will be using to grade your performance in the coming month.

Feedback: Ebay shows you the last 30 days of your feedback, broken down by *Positive, Neutral,* and *Negative.* They also give you links to leave feedback for the items you have bought and sold, as well as to automate feedback.

Shortcuts: Here, you will find links to the most popular sections on Ebay:

- Cancel bids
- End a listing
- Block bidders
- Site preferences
- Selling discussion board

- Seller Center
- Report a buyer
- Ebay Shipping Supplies
- Purchase history
- Watch list

Selling Tools: Just like the Shortcuts section, this section gives you direct links to several pages that sellers frequently use.

Selling Announcements: Links to the latest seller news from Ebay.

Promotional Offers: Links to the latest special offers just for Ebay sellers, such as any free listing promotions or store subscription offers.

Account Summary: A snapshot of your latest Ebay invoice as well as your current balance.

Research: Links to help you gain insight into your pricing, ways to improve your listings, and sourcing opportunities, including Terapeak, which I will discuss more in a bit.

(If you are overwhelmed by all these options, please do not stress; I rarely look at most of these sections myself. And you can *Personalize Your Overview* through a link at the bottom of the page, which lets you add, remove, and reorder the content shown.)

Orders: Back at the top of the *Seller Hub* page is the second tab, *Orders*. Clicking on this takes you to your pending orders that you need to ship. You can also see if you have orders that are still awaiting payment, orders that have already been shipped, cancellations, returns, and cases. You can also access the *Shipping Labels* you have already printed, which is helpful if a label did not print out correctly. Ebay makes it easy to print a second copy of the label as well as the packing slip.

Listings: The third tab at the top of *Seller Hub* is for *Listings*, and this, next to *Orders*, is the page I most frequently access. Here I can see all my *Active Listings*. There are several filters available to sort your listings as well as to edit them. Ebay shows you the number of active listings you have and the total dollar value of everything you have listed.

Marketing: The fourth tab under the *Seller Hub* is for *Marketing*. Here you can manage your store subscription, promotions, sales, and advertising. This section is a bit more advanced; we will go over it further later in this book.

Performance: The fifth tab under *Seller Hub* is *Performance*. Here you can dive deeper into your sales data. This is a relatively new feature in *Seller Hub* and one that, as of this writing, Ebay is still expanding.

Payments: The sixth tab under *Seller Hub* is another new section recently rolled out by Ebay, *Payments*. With the switch from PayPal to *Managed Payments*, this section breaks down your current financials, including your current balance, when your next payout will be, and your current invoice. You can set up when you want your payments dispersed to your bank account, daily or weekly. You can also access various reports and your taxpayer settings.

Research: The seventh and final tab under *Seller Hub* is *Research*. If you have an Ebay Store, you will be given free access to **Terapeak**, a database of the past years' worth of Ebay sales across the site. You can research what items have been selling for to price your own. While the general Ebay search gives you three months of sales data, Terapeak provides a year. Hence why having an Ebay Store is a benefit as Terapeak is included in the subscription. If you sell collectibles, you will want to access Terapeak.

My Ebay: Both Ebay buyers and sellers have a My Ebay section, which is everyone's personal Ebay page. You will see the My Ebay link at the top of Ebay's homepage. Before Ebay introduced Seller Hub, My Ebay was where you went to access all your tasks and data.

However, **My Ebay is now just for buyers.** Buyers can click on their **Activity** tab to see what items they have recently viewed, their current bids or offers, their purchase history, items on their watch lists, their saved searches, and their saved sellers.

In addition to the Activity tab, there are also tabs for **Messages** (where you can see your entire Ebay messaging system, not only messages you have received but those you have sent) and **Account** (links to some of the more popular parts of the site). As an Ebay seller, you will be using the Seller Hub to run your business, likely only accessing the My Ebay part of the site as it relates to your own purchases.

To check on your **Managed Payments** statistics, simply go to your **Seller Hub** and click on the **Payments** tab at the top of the page.

Here you will find detailed breakdowns of **Your Financial Summary**, including:

Total Funds: Here, you can see your available funds as well as pending funds. You will also see your next payout amount as well as your last payout amount. You can choose to have your money dispersed daily or weekly.

Invoice: When a buyer pays for an item, Ebay immediately deducts the selling fees. The shipping cost is also deducted after the postage is purchased. And if you have an Ebay Store, your monthly subscription fee is also deducted. Under Invoice, you will see if you have incurred any additional fees, which will show as your current amount due. You will see your last payment received and your next invoice date.

You can also *Make a one-time payment* from a third-party funding source such as your bank account, credit card, debit card, or PayPal account. Rarely do I have additional fees to pay, thanks to Managed Payments now taking care of all fees off the top. This is a significant change from when we used PayPal, as there was always a running balance to deal with.

Recent Transactions: At the bottom of the page, Ebay will show you your *Recent transactions*, including the date, order number, title, and price for each item you sold as well as the fees and shipping label charges that were taken out of your pending balance.

Settings: Under *Settings* are your current **Payout method, Payout schedule, Automatic payment method,** and **Backup payout method.** This section gives you easy access if you want to alter any of the funding/payout sources you have on file.

All Transactions: On the left-hand side of the *Payments* section of *Seller Hub* is a column of links, beginning with **All Transactions.** Clicking this link will take you to a list of the items you have sold and their associated fees. You can narrow down this information by *status, type, order number,* or a *keyword/phrase* you manually enter. You can also change the time-frame from *Last 30 days, Last 60 days, Last 90 days,* or *Custom*.

Payouts: Going back to the left-hand column, you can click on *Payouts* to see your most recent *Managed Payments* disbursements from Ebay into your bank account.

Expenses: Clicking on the *Expenses* link will take you to a list of the fees and postage costs that Ebay has recently deducted from your balance. You can break this list down further by *fee type, time range, order number,* or a *search term* of your choosing.

Reports: Back over on the left-hand column of the page, you will see *Reports*, which is where you can find a wealth of statistics regarding your business. And as a bonus, you can download these reports onto your computer to email your accountant or to print them out for your records. You can view your *Transaction Reports* or *Payout Reports*, your monthly *Statements*, and your monthly *Invoices*.

Taxes: Back over on the left-hand column, you will find the link for *Taxes*, which is where you can print out your 1099 tax forms. Note that if you sell $600 or more in a year on Ebay, Ebay will issue you a tax form. Most of us will be getting 1099 forms from both PayPal and Ebay for 2020 due to most sellers still being enrolled in PayPal and then *Managed Payments* during the year. However, remember that even if Ebay or PayPal does not issue you a tax form, you STILL need to report your IRS earnings. I will be discussing how to handle accounting for your business in the final chapter of this book.

Payout Settings: The second-to-last option on the left-hand column is your *Payout Settings*. Here you will be able to view your current settings as well as change them whenever you want. You can edit your *Payout method, Payout schedule, Automatic payment method*, and *Backup payment method*.

Taxpayer Details: The last link under the *Payments* tab is for your taxpayer settings. This section is still in BETA testing; as of this writing, it takes you to the *My Ebay* section of your account, where you can review your business information and account preferences.

Ebay is continually rolling out new features for both buyers and sellers, and the choices can seem overwhelming. As I mentioned earlier, I have my *Seller Hub* bookmarked on my computer so that I can easily access my *Orders* and *Listings*. I only check my *Payments* tab a couple of times per week in advance of my weekly payout, and I click on *Research* when I want to look up an item's price history using *Terapeak*.

As a seller, the most immediate information I need to keep up daily is my orders and listings. As you continue your Ebay journey, you can slowly begin investigating all the data Ebay provides you via your *Seller Hub*. In the beginning, focus on getting your items listed and shipped out. You will have plenty of time in the future to dig into all the statistics available to you in your *Seller Hub*.

CHAPTER THREE:

RESELLING EQUIPMENT & SUPPLIES

There are specific tools you will need to have for you to sell on Ebay successfully. I have watched far too many people attempt to sell online without having first acquired the necessary equipment. Needless to say, their Ebay businesses were short-lived. And as I have already mentioned previously in this book, I understand that it is tempting to dive head-first into reselling; however, a lot more goes into using Ebay than just listing items for sale.

Equipment: If you are going to sell on Ebay, you obviously need a **computer**. And if you are going to ship orders from home, you also need a **printer to print shipping labels**. And you will need a **camera** to take photos.

Computer: A computer with a fast processor will help you save time when creating your listings and printing your shipping labels. Either Apple or PC products are fine when selling on Ebay; it comes down to preference. You will be spending a lot of time on your computer creating Ebay listings and printing labels, so it is a vital investment in your business.

Printer: Speaking of labels: When it comes to printing shipping labels, many resellers use thermal printers. DYMO is the most well-known brand. I have always used a LaserJet printer to print my shipping labels. I tend to sell fewer items at a higher price point, so I have never felt the need to switch to a thermal printer, which can be helpful if you are shipping out dozens of orders a day. I still print my labels the old-fashioned way onto double-sided label sheets!

If you are just starting to sell on Ebay and already have a printer, use it until you see a need to upgrade to a better model. Inkjet printers use a lot of expensive ink, and you must change the cartridges frequently; hence why I use a LaserJet, which takes less ink that lasts longer.

However, if your Ebay sales increase, you may want to look into a thermal printer that prints shipping labels exclusively in rolls (the kind with the peel-off backs that you can just stick onto a package). As I mentioned, many online sellers these days use DYMO printers to print their shipping labels. There are numerous YouTube videos from resellers discussing the thermal printers they use.

Camera/Smartphone: You must put photos into your Ebay listings, so a camera is a must. When I first started reselling, I used a camera to take my Ebay photos, using the SIM card to transfer the files to my computer and then uploading them to Ebay. Now I just use my iPhone to take photos and upload them using the Ebay app. Today's smartphones take just as good, and sometimes better, pictures than digital cameras; so, if you already own a device, see if you can make it work.

The benefit of having a smartphone is that you can utilize the **Ebay App** when you are away from your computer. I use my iPhone to photograph, create drafts, and answer customer questions. I use my laptop to research, complete listings, and print shipping labels.

Computers, printers, cameras, smartphones. They all play a huge part in selling on Ebay and can be a considerable expense. Remember that any money you spend on your Ebay business equipment can be deducted as an expense come tax time. Be sure to track everything you purchase and keep the receipts so that you can claim maximum deductions. I will be discussing how to manage your Ebay accounting later in this book.

Internet Access: Fast, reliable internet access is critical to selling on Ebay. I pay $50 a month for high-speed internet access. Most phone and cable companies now offer internet services, including modems, so that you can have wireless access. Call around to the internet providers in your area and ask about any packages or specials they have for new customers. Be careful about getting locked into a long-term contract, however, and be sure you are aware of any price increases that will take place once the introductory special is over. Trust me when I say that high-speed internet is worth the price if you plan to sell a significant number of items on Ebay; you will easily be able to afford the added cost of quality internet with the additional sales you will be making!

Digital Scale: The number one supply you MUST have if you are going to sell on Ebay is a digital postal scale to weigh packages to figure out the correct postage. You can buy digital scales for around $20 to $30 on Ebay and Amazon, and they are also sold at office supply stores. Look for a "postage" specific scale that measures pounds AND ounces, as you will need to know ounces when shipping via USPS First Class mail.

You do not need a fancy digital model, just a tabletop scale that weighs ounces and pounds. I have had the same scale for over five years now; it is a small investment you MUST make if you are going to ship your Ebay orders yourself. If you are not willing to purchase a digital scale for your Ebay shipping, then be prepared to haul all your packages to the Post Office every single day, where you will wait in line and pay up for postage as they charge more at the retail counters than they do online.

I have encountered many sellers over the years who sell on Ebay without a digital postage scale. They estimate the shipping, overcharging customers in some cases (and getting negative feedback), or undercharging and losing money. Or they take all items to the Post Office BEFORE listing them to get a weight, take the packages back home, list the items, and then go BACK to the Post Office to pay for postage after the items sell. That, to me, is a HUGE waste of time and gas money, not to mention the fact that postage is more expensive at the Post Office.

Note that you get a discount on postage when you ship online at USPS.com or on Ebay. Sometimes the difference can be as much as a few dollars, and when you are shipping multiple packages, those added amounts really add up quickly!

Some sellers choose to charge a flat rate for all their orders. These sellers tend to sell the same types of items, such as postcards or clothing. For example, many clothing sellers charge $5.99 to ship clothing that weighs under one pound and ships via First Class. This results in a $1 to $3 overage depending on the weight of the package.

It is normal to pad the shipping cost a bit to cover fees and shipping supplies, but if you choose to charge a flat rate, be careful not to overcharge your customers too much. Buyers come to Ebay for deals, and the shipping charges factor into that. Savvy shoppers will know you are overcharging them on lightweight items. I will be going through the complete process to easily ship Ebay packages later in this book.

If you sell a wide variety of items in various sizes and weights, you may consider offering **Calculated Shipping**. *Calculated Shipping* charges the buyer based on the package's weight and the zip code to which it is shipping. Having a digital postal scale enables you to weigh these items before listing them to enter the correct weight. Most sellers who lose money on shipping do so because they do not weigh larger items, causing them to undercharge customers.

However, if you have a digital scale and offer *Calculated Shipping*, the buyer pays the actual shipping cost based on the package's weight and the zip code it is going to. If you have a digital scale on hand, using *Calculated Shipping* is a breeze. I will talk more about *Calculated Shipping* later in this book

Other sellers offer *free shipping*, padding the item's cost into their estimated shipping charge. While offering free shipping is a smart move for lightweight items (for instance, if you have a piece of jewelry that weighs two ounces, you can easily offer free shipping and absorb the $4 it will cost to ship), it can backfire on heavier items as buyers know when a seller has inflated the price of an item to cover shipping. You do not want to give the appearance that you are making money from the shipping costs and risk getting negative feedback.

Instead of guessing the postage costs, under-charging or over-charging, or running back and forth to the Post Office, you can save time and money by quickly printing your shipping labels from home....and a digital scale makes that possible. I will cover shipping more in-depth later in this book.

Boxes & Envelopes: You cannot just stick a label directly on a book and send it in the mail. Well, some new sellers do such things, believe it or not. Shipping packages require *shipping supplies*, and that means shipping boxes and envelopes, such as:

- Plain cardboard shipping boxes in various sizes
- USPS Priority shipping boxes
- USPS Flat Rate Priority shipping boxes
- USPS Regional Rate shipping boxes
- Poly mailers in several sizes (these are perfect for shipping clothing)

- Bubble mailers in several sizes (for shipping items that need a bit more protection than a plain poly envelope offers)
- Cardboard envelope mailers (to protect items such as coloring books and prints from being bent)

The great thing about the United States Postal Service (USPS) is that they offer FREE *Priority Mail* shipping boxes. While *Priority Mail* is an excellent option for shipping many packages, you will need other forms of packaging for *Media Mail, First Class Mail,* and *Parcel Select,* as well as for international shipments (again, more on these forms of shipping coming up). Basically, you need two forms of shipping boxes/envelopes: *Priority Mail* boxes and envelopes, and plain boxes and envelopes for the rest.

USPS Standard Priority Boxes:

- **Priority Mail Show Box SHOEBOX:** 14-7/8 x 7-3/8 x 5.24 (not just for shoes, but for anything long and narrow)
- **Priority Mail Box 1097**: 11-5/8 x 2.5x 13-7/16 (rectangle size for clothing, books, and anything flat)
- **Priority Mail Box 1905:** 12.5 x 3-1/8 x 15-5/8 (rectangle size for clothing, books, and anything flat)
- **Priority Mail Box 1092**: 12.25 x 2-7/8 x 13-11/16 (rectangle size for clothing, books, and anything flat)
- **Priority Mail Box 1096L**: 9-7/16 x 6-7/16 x 2-3/16 (rectangle size for clothing, books, and anything flat)
- **Large Priority Mail Box 7**: 12.25 x 12.25 x 1.5 (largest size of the Priority Mail boxes; perfect for shipping several items at once)
- **Priority Mail Box 4**: 7.25 x 7.25 x 6.25 (square size is perfect for shipping mugs, figurines, and small, rounded items)

USPS Flat-Rate Priority Boxes & Envelopes:

- **Priority Mail Padded Flat Rate Envelope**: 9.5 x 12.5 (the go-to choice for shipping heavy clothing, shoes, and anything unbreakable)
- **Priority Mail Small Flat Rate Box**: 8-11/16 x 5-7/16 x 1.75 (sized for small but heavy items)
- **Priority Mail Medium Flat Rate Box 1**: 11.25 x 8.75 x 6 (perfect size for mid-size, heavy objects)
- **Priority Mail Medium Flat Rate Box 2**: 12 x 3.5 x 14-1/8 (the flat, rectangle version of the size above)
- **Priority Mail Large Flat Rate Box LARGEFRB**: 12.25 x 12.25 x 6 (this box is smaller than the regular Large Priority Mail Box, but it can still come in handy for smaller, heavier items)
- **Priority Mail Regional Rate Box A1**: 10-1/8 x 7-1/8 x 5 (postage for the Regional Rate boxes are often cheaper than their regular Flat Rate counterparts)
- **Priority Rate Regional Rate Box A2**: 11-1/16 x 2.5 x 13-1/16 (the rectangle version of the Regional Rate A1 box)

USPS Priority Stickers: (*these are perfect for covering writing on the outside of repurposed boxes*)

- **Priority Mail Sticker Label 107 Roll of 250**
- **Priority Mail Sticker Label 107R Roll of 1000**
- **Priority Mail Shipping Label 106 Pack of 10**

When you are looking through all the available choices for *Priority Mail* boxes and envelopes, you will see that USPS offers many other options that I did not list above. As you continue along your Ebay journey, you will learn which shipping boxes and envelopes you use the most, and therefore, you need to reorder frequently. While the above selections are the products most resellers use most, here are some other ones you may want to consider adding to your supply as you grow your business:

- **Priority Mail Express Boxes & Envelopes**: I do not offer Express or Overnight options to my customers (and I have only ever had one person ask me to ship something faster than Priority), so for me, I do not bother keeping any of these products stocked. If I needed to send something via Express, I would likely just take it to the Post Office packaged in a plain box and have them put the label and Express stickers on it. However, these options do exist if you decide to offer them.
- **Tube Boxes:** If you sell posters and/or prints, these long triangular tube boxes work great.
- **Envelopes:** There are several options for flat envelopes, but whenever I want to send something that would fit in one of these options, I ship it in a Padded Flat Rate. These envelopes are geared toward businesses that frequently mail documents, such as law, banking, and medical offices.
- **Regional Rate Boxes:** For me, Regional Rate A boxes are always the cheapest option. The B boxes' benefit is that they can ship up to 20-pounds, while the A boxes hold a maximum of 15-pounds for domestic shipments. However, I have never had to ship anything that heavy that actually fit in any of the Regional Rate boxes, regardless.

The Post Office offers its free shipping supplies in quantities as low as ten each. I recommend that you order the smallest number possible as you expand your collection. You will soon realize which boxes you use the most, but you will at least have the others on hand if you need them.

Note that sometimes it can take quite a while for boxes to be delivered due to supply issues; so, do not wait until you are completely out to order more, especially heading into the busy holiday season. I make sure I order my supply of *Priority Mail* boxes in September in anticipation of the fourth quarter.

While *Priority Mail* is an excellent option for shipping most packages, you will need other forms of packaging for **Media Mail, First Class Mail,** and **Parcel Select,** as those selections can NOT be mailed in the *Priority Mail* boxes. It is also against USPS policy to alter the *Priority* boxes in any way, so forget thinking you can turn them inside out (they are printed with *Priority Mail* on the inside to thwart this) or put stickers on the outside to conceal the fact that they are indeed *Priority*. Misusing USPS supplies can result in your losing your postal account.

Before you run out and buy new shipping boxes and envelopes, check around your house to see what you have on hand. Plain cardboard boxes, manila envelopes, and bubble mailers can all be used for non-priority mail. If you already have items on hand that you intend to list on Ebay, look them over to determine the packaging you need. Perhaps you are only going to sell books, for which bubble mailers and sturdy boxes are enough. On the other hand, if you only plan to sell large items, you do not need to worry about stocking up on envelopes.

I keep a wide variety of boxes and envelopes in my shipping supply area. While I utilize the free *Priority Mail* boxes and bubble mailers from the Post Office, I invest in plain shipping boxes from Amazon, Ebay, Uline, and Value Mailers for *Media, First Class,* and *Parcel* packages; and I purchase branded shipping supplies directly from Ebay. I also have manila bubble mailer envelopes that I buy at Sam's Club and poly mailers that I order on Amazon. I keep the following plain boxes and envelopes on hand:

- **Plain Cardboard Shipping Boxes** (4", 6", 8", 10", and 12" sizes)
- **Oversized Cardboard Shipping Boxes** (14" and 16" sizes for when I have to ship oversized items via Parcel

or UPS)
- **Poly Mailers in various sizes** (for shipping clothing)
- **Bubble Mailers in various sizes** (for items that need more cushioning than a plain poly mailer)
- **Cardboard Mailers in various sizes** (for shipping coloring books, stickers, and other items that I do not want bent in the mail)

Note that because I have been selling on Ebay for years and am set up as a business, I can buy these supplies and then deduct them as business expenses. As you begin to purchase more shipping supplies and office equipment, be sure to track your spending, as you can deduct these costs come tax time. Therefore, I try to limit the places I buy supplies from as I can simply scan my credit card statements to find my monthly expenses.

Packing Materials: You cannot just throw an item into a box and ship it with no packing materials to buffer it inside of the box (well, you CAN, as I have seen many sellers do, but you should not). You need to WRAP up your items to protect them inside of the box. You want to ensure that the item is protected from being thrown around, both inside of planes and trucks, as well as being tossed onto customer's porches. I invest in the following packing materials for my Ebay orders:

- **Recycled Packing Paper** (to wrap up items inside of the shipping box)
- **Bubble Wrap** (essential for protecting breakables such as China and ceramics)
- **Packing Peanuts** (perfect for buffering breakables inside of boxes)
- **Shipping Tape** (buy the largest rolls and the strongest type you can)
- **Tissue Paper** (better than packing paper for wrapping delicate breakables)
- **Cardboard Corrugated Rolls** (allows you to create a

box-in-a-box around breakables)

Since I have an established Ebay business, I invest in **recycled white or gray packing paper** to wrap up the items to arrive neatly packaged inside the shipping box. However, I also use **newspapers** to protect the item further. Do NOT wrap your item in the newspaper directly; you do not want any newspaper ink to bleed onto your products. Also, make sure any newspaper you do use is clean.

In addition to packing paper, I also purchase **bubble wrap** to protect fragile items. In my area, I have found Sam's Club to have the best price on bubble wrap; Costco also carries it at the same price.

Bubble wrap is a MUST for protecting ceramics such as coffee mugs (which I sell many!). After the item is wrapped securely in bubble wrap, I then use the newspaper to buffer it inside the box further so that the newspaper ink does not bleed directly onto the item itself. If it is a breakable item, we also go a step further and surround the piece with a **cardboard wrap** OVER the bubble wrap; this creates a "box in a box" effect that further protects the item.

Packing peanuts are always nice to have on hand to use in shipments, but buying them new is expensive. I save any that I get from my own online orders, and I let my friends and family know that I will gladly take their unwanted packing peanuts off their hands. Most people are happy to get rid of the packing peanuts as they are a static mess to deal with and cannot be recycled.

When I do purchase packing peanuts, I buy them in bulk to save money. I also have a large plastic container on wheels, which was marketed to hold dog food, and I store the peanuts inside. A large slotted scoop (I use one intended for scooping cat litter!) makes transferring the peanuts from the container into the shipping box quick and easy.

Another shipping supply staple I keep on hand is **tissue paper**. Ebay sells its own branded tissue paper, and I also buy any that I find at estate sales. Sam's Club and Costco usually both sell huge rolls of tissue paper, particularly around Christmas, and after the holidays, if there is any left, you can get it on clearance.

Tissue paper is essential for cushioning small, fragile items such as porcelain figurines and jewelry. Since it is much thinner than newspaper or packing paper, it tucks nicely into small curves to protect delicate pieces during shipment. Tissue paper is also nice for wrapping up designer pieces of clothing. Of course, after I wrap something fragile in tissue paper, I also wrap it in bubble wrap and use other packing materials to protect it further.

Shipping Tape: So, you now have boxes, envelopes, packing paper, newspaper, bubble wrap, and maybe even some packing peanuts, cardboard rolls, and tissue paper. To seal your packages, you need shipping tape.

Clear shipping tape can be found at drugstores, big-box retailers, office supply stores, warehouse clubs, and even dollar stores. I purchase my shipping tape at Sam's Club. Dollar for dollar, I find it to be the best quality and the best price. Costco also sells shipping tape in bulk.

Note that you want to *purchase SHIPPING tape, not packing tape.* Packing tape is for moving boxes and is not as strong, while shipping tape is meant to hold packages together as they travel to their destination by vehicle, boat, and/or air.

I also have a **handheld tape dispenser** (usually sold right next to the tape at stores). If you are starting out, I recommend buying a kit with the tape dispenser included and some extra tape rolls. You can usually find such kits for $10 to $15 in the tape section of the big box stores. You only need to buy the dispenser once and then tape refills as needed. Periodically throughout the year, the shipping tape at Sam's Club and Costco goes on sale; and when it does, I stock up.

Ebay also sells branded shipping tape. If you have an Ebay Store subscription of *Basic* or higher, you may want to use your quarterly shipping supplies coupon toward some of this tape. Not only is it great for sealing up packages, but it also acts as a sticker when you need to cover up writing that may be on repurposed shipping boxes.

Enclosures: I strongly believe in putting enclosures into my shipments; I personally include a **packing slip** and a **business card sized "thank you" card** in all my packages.

Not all Ebay sellers agree, however; some do not put anything into their shipments. So, whether to include enclosures is a decision you will have to make for yourself. If you sell similar items, such as certain collectibles or clothing brands, you may find it advantageous to encourage repeat buyers, and enclosures can help you do that.

However, if you just sell a wide variety of random stuff, you may not be as concerned with leaving your customers with any impression of your store. I have personally worked hard to create a "brand" for my Ebay Store, and I promote that "brand" via my packing slips and enclosure cards.

If you do decide to include packing slips in your orders, Ebay makes it super easy to do as after you print a shipping label, there is a link you can click on to print a packing slip. The packing slip is just a copy of the original invoice sent to the customer when they purchased the item.

I must admit that when I first started selling on Ebay, I did not want to include a packing slip as I did not want to spend the money on ink and paper. Fortunately, I was able to chat with some experienced Ebay sellers who convinced me that including a packing slip was vital in maintaining a professional image. When I order something online, I am put off if there is not a packing slip inside. So why should I treat my Ebay customers any differently? When running my business, I adhere to the Golden Rule and treat my customers how I would want to be treated.

In addition to a packing slip, I also include enclosure cards in my shipments. Over the years, these have ranged from business cards to large postcards. No matter the size, the card always THANKS the customer for their purchase. I order these enclosure cards from VistaPrint.com, which allows me to create professional business materials at a great price easily. Other places that sell business cards are Moo, GotPrint, JukeBox, USP Store, Staples, and Office Max/Office Depot.

If you are just starting out selling on Ebay, I recommend that you include a packing slip and perhaps write "Thank You!" on it to give it a personal touch. If you decide that you want to make Ebay a real part-time or even a full-time business, you can look into having enclosure cards printed up. The choice, however, is totally up to you.

Shipping Station: Now that you have all your shipping supplies, you need a place to prepare your shipments. If you have space, it is nice to designate an area just for shipping out your orders. Although, as many times as I have tried to keep all my shipping supplies in one location, inevitably, they wind up scattered between several places in my house!

I keep all my shipping boxes and poly bags in my basement, which is where my Ebay inventory is stored. When an item sells, I retrieve it from my inventory, and the box or envelope it will ship out in. I then take both the item and shipping container back upstairs to my office to be weighed so that I can print out the shipping label and packing slip.

I have a table in my office where my digital scale always sits at the ready. It is right next to my computer to weigh items as I am listing them and again when I am ready to print the shipping label. The most important thing is to have your digital scale on a flat surface so that you can get an accurate reading. I use the scale both when I am listing items and again when I go to ship them. When I bring an item up to my office to be shipped, I weigh it and print the label and packing slip.

After I have printed the label and packing slip, I take the package to my dad, who handles all my Ebay shipping; his official title is the "Shipping & Receiving Manager"! He loves his "job," and it keeps him busy in his retirement. My dad keeps his packing supplies on a wheeled cart next to a large table. The cart holds tissue paper, packing paper, tape, scissors, and various other shipping supplies, such as a box cutter and Scotch tape. He keeps bubble wrap and the container of packing peanuts next to the table to have everything within his reach to package up orders.

I have shelving in the basement and in my office for all my boxes, envelopes, packing materials, and tape. Again, since I have an established business, I have a lot of shipping materials; and since I own a home, I have a lot of space to store it all. However, if you are just starting out, use an out-of-the-way space (perhaps in the basement or in the corner of a room) for your shipping supplies. You want to make sure your supplies (and the items you are selling) are away from any smoke, pets, or other household odors. Yes, customers WILL complain if they find dog hair inside their packages; and cigarette smoke complaints can lead to negative feedback.

Your shipping area is just as important as your inventory space, so take the time to set it up properly. A well-organized shipping station will save you time and money in the long run, as will making sure you have the right equipment and supplies at the ready before you list your first item for sale on Ebay.

CHAPTER FOUR:

WHAT TO SELL & WHERE TO SOURCE

The most common question I get from people interested in reselling is, "What sells on Ebay?" There is no easy answer to this because, for every item that sells well on Ebay, ten more do not. There are hundreds of thousands of Ebay listings and millions of registered users. Learning what sells and what does not sell takes time and lots of trial and error.

I have been selling on Ebay for nearly two decades, and I am still shocked at what sells for me. Similarly, I also pick up things that I am sure will sell but that, for whatever reason, do not. As I always tell people, "An item is only worth what someone is willing to pay for it." And there are millions of things that no one is interested in paying money for.

As I have already discussed, the best place to find items to start selling on Ebay is your own home. In fact, when I first got started on Ebay in 2005, I started by selling unused items in my house. I quickly made $3,000 by selling my old clothes (business casual attire I had accumulated from seven years of office work), books, CDs, DVDs, and housewares. These were all items I usually would have donated to Goodwill or sold for pennies on the dollar at a garage sale, but by taking a bit of extra time to list them on Ebay, I got a considerable amount of money for them.

If you are interested in specific lists of items that I have personally sold on Ebay, be sure to check out my books **101 ITEMS TO SELL ON EBAY** and **101 MORE ITEMS TO SELL ON EBAY**, both of which are available on Amazon. But to get started, look around your house for the following items:

- CDs
- DVDs and Blu-Rays
- Books
- Name-brand clothing and accessories
- Unused cosmetics
- Home décor from upscale stores such as Pottery Barn
- Tools
- Figurines
- Ceramics
- Dishes
- Flatware
- Anything licensed such as Disney, Peanuts, or Harry Potter
- Toys, both new and vintage
- Office supplies such as unopened printer ink and printer cartridges
- Craft supplies
- Small appliances
- Unused pet supplies
- Unopened gourmet food

These are just a handful of the categories of items that you can sell on Ebay. The longer you sell on the site, the more you will discover what things sell (and do not sell) online. Before you know it, you will not be able to browse in a store without wondering if you could sell their items on Ebay. Believe me when I tell you that most resellers have a tough time shopping for themselves as they view everything they see as something they could potentially sell online.

And, here is the part of the book I know many of you have been anxiously waiting to get to: **WHERE exactly can you find products to sell on Ebay?** Well, grab a pen so that you can write down the directions to the Ebay warehouse in Ohio that sells millions of items you can buy to resell online!

Please do not tell me you reached for a pen, because I was joking! When I joined Ebay in 2005, this was a popular joke that experienced sellers said to newbies on the message boards. I just had to include it here!

Unfortunately, there is no conveniently located warehouse or website where you can order products for cheap and make a significant profit on them on Ebay. If there were, everyone who sold on Ebay would be ordering from them.

Sourcing products to resell is WORK; it is probably the HARDEST part of selling on Ebay. It is also the most addicting part of reselling, as the business attracts people who love to thrift shop. History is filled with many people who wanted to start reselling but instead found themselves with a shopping addiction and a hoard of unlisted items. Shopaholics and hoarders beware: Ebay is NOT the business for you!

Fortunately, for those who are disciplined about sourcing and listings, there are millions of items available to sell and lots of places to look for them. No one is ever going to tell you where THEY are getting their items, though, and it is terribly tacky to ask. Why would someone tell you where they are finding items to resell and make you their competition?

Here are the general locations, however, in which you can find items to resell:

Garage Sales, Estate Sales, and Thrift Stores: Selling secondhand items, whether they are collectibles or clothing, is a hot business model on Ebay. It has been my method of reselling for over half of my Ebay career.

The great thing about "picking" is that you always have a source of items. Even if you live in an area with brutal winters when no one has garage sales, you can still find items to resell at thrift stores. Sourcing thrifted products are the least risky as the start-up cost is minimal. You can quickly start earning money just by spending $20 on a shopping bag full of thrift finds. The trick, of course, is to buy the right items at the right price. And that comes with time and practice.

Clearance Racks at Retail Stores: If you love to browse the big box stores and shops at your local shopping mall, finding brand new, not secondhand, items to resell on Ebay may be right up your alley. Again, it is all about finding the right items for the right price. This type of "picking" is called "retail arbitrage," and it works best if you have a smartphone that will allow you to look up items on Ebay before you buy them to resell.

Ebay offers a completed listing search (as well as Terapeak Research for Ebay Store subscribers) that enables you to see if the game you found for 75% off is selling online. I typically only purchase store clearance items that are 90% off to resell on Ebay. Remember that people shop on Ebay looking for deals, so it is unlikely you will be able to sell new items for their full retail price. And since many other resellers are also sourcing clearance items to flip, there is a lot of competition. However, sometimes adding in a few items you have scored via retail arbitrage can help bring in traffic to your other listings.

Liquidation: Many people assume that "wholesale" and "liquidation" are the same, but they are entirely different. While wholesale companies deal in brand new items directly from the manufacturer, liquidation companies directly source their products from retail stores where the items did not sell. A retailer buys from a wholesaler, but any inventory that does not sell (including returns or damaged products), is sold by the retailer to liquidation companies. Liquidation companies then sell to resellers, not only those who sell online but also people who sell at flea markets and in their own brick-and-mortar stores.

Liquidation sources are closely guarded as competition is fierce among online resellers. And when you are first starting out selling on Ebay, it is not something you should invest in until you truly understand how reselling works.

If you decide to look into liquidation, it is vital to educate yourself on each liquidation company you consider purchasing from. Find out their terms and precisely what types of products they are selling. Liquidation is usually rated as **Salvage, Customer Returns, Shelf Pulls,** or **Brand New.**

Salvage items, also referred to as *Scratch & Dent,* often come with some damage level, even if it is just to the outside packaging. *Customer Returns* may come to you without the original tags attached or some spots such as makeup on them. *Shelf Pulls* are products that were out for sale on the store shelves but were then pulled for liquidation. While these items are considered new, they may have shelf wear, including torn packaging. Items marketed as *New* may, in fact, be *Shelf Pulls,* so you must understand precisely how the liquidation company you are dealing with is grading their items.

I only buy liquidation lots labeled as brand new and that have a manifest, which is a detailed list of every product included in the lot along with the original retail price. Most companies will still warn you that even brand-new lots can contain up to 10% of items that have damage. Just as buying items at wholesale requires a lot of homework, so does purchasing liquidation!

If you sell on Ebay, you already know that thrift stores and garage sales are where most resellers find the items they sell. Buying items secondhand for pennies on the dollar will always net you the greatest return on investment. But if you want to try out liquidation, here are some of the biggest companies that cater to resellers:

B&G Trading: B&G Trading specializes in overstock, shelf-pull, and liquidation clothing from Macy's and Nordstrom's. They sell by both the case and the pallet.

Bstock.Com: B-Stock connects you directly with liquidation sources at Amazon, Best Buy, Game Stop, GE, Lowe's, Macy's, Office Depot/Office Max, QVC, Walmart, Whirlpool, Sears, and JCPenney. Most of the sites they connect to are selling truckloads of merchandise via auction.

Bulq.com: Bulq.com sells liquidation from Target, Lowe's, and Bed Bath & Beyond, but most of their items come from Target. They offer both cases and pallets with conditions of Brand New, Like New, Salvage, Scratch & Dent, and Uninspected Returns. Shipping on cases is $30; shipping on pallets is $200. They put up new lots every day, and they continuously mark them down until they sell. Bulq.com is an excellent source for cosmetics, toys, and consumer electronics.

Note that Bulq.com has recently partnered with Ebay to sell their liquidation lots directly on the Ebay site. The benefit to this is that when you purchase a lot from Bulq on Ebay, the manifest immediately creates drafts of everything in the case. This is extremely helpful in starting the listing process. However, it is essential to note that the photos in their manifests do not migrate to the drafts. Plus, not all the listing details will be correct. You will still need to double-check the listings and provide your own photos.

Continental Wholesale: Located in Iowa, Continental Wholesale offers truckloads, half truckloads, and pallet lots of store liquidation from sixteen different retailers.

Direct Liquidation: Direct Liquidation offers products from major retailers such as Walmart, Target, Lowe's, and Amazon in the form of auctions. They sell by the box, pallet, and truckload.

EBAY: You are selling on Ebay, but did you know you can source on Ebay, too? There are hundreds of liquidation lots for sale on Ebay at any given time. Just search "liquidation" or "reseller box" to see what is currently for sale.

ETSY: If you want to buy vintage items or craft supplies in bulk to resell, try Etsy. Sellers are advertising "wholesale" and "reseller lots" of all sorts.

Fox Liquidation: Fox Liquidation advertises wholesale clothing from brands such as Ralph Lauren, DKNY, Lacoste, Tommy Hilfiger, and more. They call their cases "small wholesale lots" and their pallets "wholesale lots." Their website also features a clearance section.

Goodwill Bluebox: In 2019, Goodwill launched their "Bluebox" website, which sells lots of clothing that did not sell in stores and was headed to one of their outlet locations. As of this writing, Goodwill Bluebox is very new, and they sell out almost instantly whenever new stock launches. Hopefully, they will grow the program as it is an affordable way to source potential Ebay inventory. It is worth signing up for their email list and following them on Instagram for inventory updates.

Honcho Wholesale: Honcho Wholesale offers liquidation by the case and pallet. They mainly focus on clothing from Macy's, Nordstrom, and Nordstrom Rack. All their lots are fully manifested so that you know exactly what you are buying.

Liquidation.com: Liquidation.com offers a massive variety of goods to resell, including clothing, jewelry, electronics, computers, housewares, tools, and general merchandise. The twist is that the lots come from different sellers from across the country and are primarily available at auction. If you like hunting for deals, you will love scrolling through Liquidation.com in search of lots to bid on.

Liquidation General: Liquidation General specializes in high-end department store clothing. They also sell jewelry and specialty lots. Shipping on most of their lots appears to be free.

Merchandize Liquidators: Merchandize Liquidators specializes in truckloads and pallets of cosmetics, clothing, housewares, and more. You can visit their headquarters in Miami Gardens, Florida, or buy from them online.

MidTenn Wholesale: Run by former Ebay sellers, MidTenn Wholesale sells a variety of merchandise from various sources in conditions ranging from brand new to salvage. Their lots are at a fixed price and range from cases to truckloads.

POSHMARK: Poshmark is an app (it is also accessible via computer) where people can buy and sell clothing. There is a whole community of Poshmark resellers, and some of them also offer wholesale/liquidation lots for sale. Try typing "liquidation," "wholesale," or "reseller lot" into the search bar to see what is available. Since Poshmark offers flat $6.95 Priority Mail shipping on packages weighing five pounds or less, expect only to find smaller lots for sale. But, again, it is an affordable way to test liquidation or buying in bulk.

Quicklotz.com: Quicklotz offers cases, pallets, and truckloads at set prices that ship from three warehouses across the United States. They also sell Mystery Cases that ship for free within the Continental United States.

ThredUP: While not a traditional liquidation company, ThredUP, an online consignment store, sells "Rescue" boxes. These mystery box lots contain items that were not accepted for consignment or items that they had listed but did not sell. They offer clothing, handbags, shoes, and jewelry.

ViaTrading: With lots starting at only $100, ViaTrading is an excellent option for testing out liquidation. They sell everything from brand new cosmetics to salvage appliances. If you are in the Los Angeles, California, area, you can even visit their warehouse and purchase pallets in person. They also have weekly on-site auctions.

Wholesale Ninjas: Wholesale Ninjas sells liquidation by the case, pallet, and truckload. They mainly sell cosmetics, toys, and clothing from Target and CVS. With box lots starting at around $100, Wholesale Ninjas offers an affordable way to test liquidation.

Ebay Wholesale Deals: If you have an Ebay Store subscription, you can access the Ebay Wholesale Deals via the Manage My Store section under Subscriber discounts. Ebay Wholesale Deals is an exclusive marketplace where Ebay Store subscribers can buy new or refurbished merchandise in wholesale quantities.

Consignment: Another popular Ebay business model is to sell items on consignment for other people. The great thing about consignment is that you do not have to buy any products to re-sell yourself, so your financial risk is very low. However, selling on consignment is not for a newbie Ebay seller. You need to have a firm understanding of how to use Ebay because you, yourself, have already been selling on the site. You also need to be able to deal effectively with people, especially being able to let them down easily when they show you a pile of junk that you know will not sell on Ebay.

Most people who sell on consignment take at least a 50% commission fee (although I have seen it as high as 80%), and out of that comes all the Ebay fees and related expenses (office supplies, shipping materials). You also must take responsibility for other people's items; having extra insurance to cover those things when they are in your possession is necessary but will cost more money.

However, if you are a people person, already know how to sell on Ebay, have a passion for antiques and collectibles, and like the idea of not having to personally source products, then selling on consignment might be for you.

CHAPTER FIVE:

RESELLING CLOTHING

This chapter is for those of you who are wanting to sell clothing on Ebay, whether you simply want to add in a bit or it is the only category you want to sell in. Clothing is different from reselling hard goods, hence why I've devoted a chapter specifically to it.

Why is clothing such a great item to sell on Ebay? Not only are secondhand clothes highly sought after by buyers on Ebay (it is the number one category on the site), but clothing is extremely easy and cheap for sellers to find for resale. Garage sales, yard sales, rummage sales, estate sales, charity sales, consignment stores, and thrift stores are all bursting at the seams with clothes. No matter what the climate is where you live, you can always find clothing somewhere in your area to buy for resale on Ebay!

Clothes to resell can be found in numerous places, including:

Thrift Stores: My favorite place to buy clothing to resell in my area is Goodwill. The Goodwill stores in my area usually have one half-off day every month and sometimes even have dollar days where all items in their stores, including clothing, are only $1. Since the few store shopping carts available get snatched up immediately, I bring my own collapsible cart. Having a cart is essential when shopping at thrift stores for clothing because carrying around a pile of clothes is extremely difficult. While one piece of clothing may be lightweight, a pile of them together is heavy!

When I am at Goodwill, I quickly search through the racks looking for my favorite styles and brands (tips on what to look for coming up later in this chapter). My goal is to get through the clothing racks as quickly as possible to snag the best stuff. Not only am I competing with the regular shoppers, but I am also in a race against the other resellers in the store who are doing the same thing I am.

You likely have Goodwill locations in your area, but there are many other secondhand stores across the country. From large chains such as Savers and Value Village to locally run Salvation Army stores and other charity shops, search out all the thrift shops in your city to find which ones are worth sourcing clothing at.

While all thrift stores are managed differently, most do have discount days or other sale promotions. However, not all advertise their sales. You need to be proactive and ask the clerks about any sale days or discount cards. Many stores also have social media accounts, so find the locations near you on Facebook and Instagram to keep up with their sales announcements. And be sure to check their websites for sale calendars and email lists you can sign up for so that you do not miss any special offers.

You want to make sure you are paying as little as possible for clothing as it is a crowded market on Ebay. The regular everyday prices at my Goodwill are too high for me to make a profit on, so I must shop during the sales. As with any item you are buying to resell, you want to buy low and sell high (i.e., buy it CHEAP and sell it for a big PROFIT!).

Goodwill Outlets: Goodwill has pay-by-the-pound outlet stores in some markets, also referred to as "The Bins." The outlet stores sell merchandise that did not sell in the regular Goodwill locations. Sometimes, if an area has an abundance of donations, items skip the regular stores altogether and go straight to the outlets.

Most Goodwill Outlet stores use big plastic blue bins on rollers to bring merchandise out onto the sales floor, hence the nickname "The Bins." Shoppers must dig through these giant bins to find what they want to buy; at checkout, they roll their shopping carts onto a big scale to see how much they have purchased in weight (minus the shopping cart as the stores calibrate their scales to account for the heavy metal carts).

Every Goodwill Outlet location is run differently. Some charge the same per-pound rate for all items, while others separate clothing from hard goods. Some locations only sell clothing, and others sell a mix of both clothes and hard goods such as books, dishes, toys, and décor. Some outlets are very clean and orderly; some are a dusty, dirty mess.

Condition is a huge issue when sourcing clothing at the Goodwill Outlets. Again, most of the pieces were for sale first in a regular Goodwill store but did not sell there, hence why they were sent to "The Bins." There may be a reason that an item did not sell at the regular store, such as it perhaps had a stain or tear.

Garage Sales: In addition to thrift stores and "The Bins," you can also find clothing at garage sales, yard sales, tag sales, and rummage sales, which are all the same thing but seem to be called something different depending on the area of the country you live in. As a reseller, I used to cringe when I would drive up to a garage sale and see racks of clothing. However, now I know that garages full of clothing can be gold mines.

In my city, garage sales are advertised in the local newspaper as well as on Facebook. Several Facebook groups are dedicated to posting local garage sales online, and some cities even post their sales on mobile apps. And some people skip the ads altogether and just put signs up when they are having a sale.

Garage "sail-ing" usually requires a lot of driving from house to house looking for treasures, but for those who love hunting deals, garage sales can pay off big time. A bit of planning the night before you go out is essential; I create a map of the advertised sales and always end up finding unadvertised ones, too, as I am driving around my area.

When hitting up garage sales, be sure to have a lot of cash on hand, mostly $1 and $5 bills. If you are buying clothing, try bundling several pieces together and asking for a deal. While getting to sales early means you get the best selection, showing up toward the end of the sale might pay off if the homeowners are desperate to unload their unsold items. If you go to a sale and the prices are too high on their opening day, try going back during their last hour to see if they are willing to sell to you at a discount.

Charity Sales: Charity sales are held everywhere, from churches and schools to community centers and senior homes. Since multiple people are usually donating goods to these sales, they attract huge crowds. Most charity sales I have been to sell clothing for $1 apiece or by-the-bag for $5.

Since charity sales tend to attract many shoppers, I try to make sure I am in line early to score the best deals. However, it can also be advantageous to attend on the last day of these sales as many organizations are desperate to sell all remaining items and may offer discounts, including fill-a-bag deals. Most charity sales are cash only, so be sure you are ready with $1 and $5 bills.

Estate Sales: Estate sales are usually held by professional liquidation companies and are in the homes of someone who is moving or has passed away. While most people go to estate sales searching for antiques and collectibles, many estate sales also have clothing. If it is an estate of an older person, you may luck out and find vintage clothes. I love finding vintage jackets and hats at estate sales.

Research all the estate sale companies in your area and start attending their sales so that you learn how they price their items. Most also have Facebook pages where they post photos of their sales. Also, find out what payments they accept; in my area, some only accept cash and checks while others only accept cash and credit cards. Some companies may want you to bring your own bags and provide your own manpower, while others insist on bagging your items for you and carrying them to your car.

Be friendly and get to know the staff. Remember that estate sale companies are working for the homeowners while also paying their own business expenses. Often, they are not willing to negotiate prices, especially on the first day. However, most companies do offer remaining items at half-off on the last day or in the final hours. Usually, the more you buy, the more they are willing to negotiate with you.

Consignment Stores: Whether it is a big chain store or a small local operation, consignment stores are typically full of clothing. While prices can be high on the newest items put out on the sales floor, the longer an item sits, the more it gets discounted. Plus, most stores have frequent sales. Visit the consignment stores in your area to learn about their pricing and sale calendars, as well as to see what sorts of merchandise they sell. Also, see if they have social media pages, specifically on Facebook, that you can follow for updates.

Plato's Closet and Buffalo Exchange are two national consignment stores that focus on trendy clothing for younger people. Both stores buy items outright from patrons who bring in their unwanted clothing. Our Plato's Closet has frequent sales, discounting pieces as low as 90%. Some stores offer dollar days and even fill-a-bag sales. Again, find your local store on social media so that you can keep up-to-date with their sales and promotions.

Facebook Marketplace: "For Sale" ads used to be placed in local newspapers, but these days many people sell their items on Facebook Marketplace. I often see people selling lots of clothing (usually in a specific size as they are cleaning out their closets) for next to nothing. While you will likely end up with some pieces that you cannot resell due to style or condition, it is a quick and easy way to get a large amount of inventory, which is especially nice if you are just starting to resell clothing.

Facebook is also a great place to advertise that you are looking to purchase clothing in bulk. Be sure to specify the brands, styles, and/or sizes you are looking for and what you are willing to pay. Also, be clear that you only purchase from smoke-free homes. When meeting people from Facebook to buy items, stay safe, and choose a public place during the daytime. If possible, take someone with you, again, just to be safe.

Friends & Family: Let your friends and family know that you are looking to purchase any clothing they want to part with. Posting this to your Facebook page is a great way to spread the word. Be ready with a list of the brands, sizes, and styles you are looking for, along with how much you are willing to pay for each piece. Have this information firmly established so that you do not get guilt-tripped into buying items you do not want to resell, such as kids' clothing or small-sized tops from Walmart.

So, we have established that secondhand clothing is available no matter where you live, and you now know it can be had for cheap. However, just because clothing is easy and inexpensive to source does not mean you should buy it all up to resell on Ebay.

Style, size, condition, and brand name all factor into how much an item will sell for or if it will even sell at all.

Clothing Categories: Clothing covers a wide variety of categories on Ebay, from accessories and shoes to outerwear and underwear. Here are just some of the categories of clothing that you can sell on Ebay:

Belts: Resellers often overlook the belt category, but there is a market for belts on Ebay. Look for higher-end brand names as well as larger sizes; genuine leather pieces sell best.

Blazers: Both women's and men's blazers (also called suit jackets) are expensive to purchase new, which is why many shoppers turn to Ebay to find them secondhand at a great price. When sourcing blazers, be sure to check that all the buttons are intact, including those on the cuffs.

Bras: Bras in large sizes and from popular brands, such as Victoria's Secret, sell very well on Ebay. I used to cringe when I saw a table full of bras at a garage sale, but now I kick myself for passing them by!

Coats & Jackets: I love to pick up coats and jackets in the offseason when no one else is looking at them. I focus on better brand names and larger sizes, and I double-check all buttons, zippers, and linings to ensure there are no missing pieces or flaws. I also look to see if the coat initially had a detachable hood; I pass up many coats that end up having their hoods missing. The same goes for missing belts on trench coats.

Corduroy Jackets: Be careful to differentiate between denim and corduroy jackets in your listings; I once described a corduroy jacket as denim and had to accept a return on it. While both corduroy and denim are usually 100% cotton and have the same structure, corduroy, which is thick and textured, has a much different feel than denim.

Denim Jackets: Blue jean denim jackets have always been my best-selling clothing item. They are the one item where the brand does not matter as much as any good-looking jacket seems to sell well. Denim jackets in colors other than blue (such as black, red, or pink) are incredibly hot on Ebay, as are coats in larger sizes. Note the fabric makeup when listing jean jackets as some have stretch via spandex, which is a feature many customers want.

Dresses: New dresses are expensive and are an item that many people only wear once, which is why so many shoppers turn to Ebay to find their special occasion dresses at a discount. However, do not just focus on sourcing formal dresses as casual summer dresses and career wear dresses sell just as well, and sometimes even better.

Handbags: You will likely find purses, totes, and wallets displayed near the clothing at most thrift stores. Look for brand-name bags with little to no wear (including on the inside) to flip on Ebay. Check to ensure the zippers work and that all details, such as studs and jewels, are intact.

Many bags were initially sold with detachable cross-body straps; if you pick up a purse that is missing this extra strap, it can still sell; make sure you disclose that the strap is missing. Also, look over the bag's interior lining; this is where I often find the most issues as the linings are often dirty and stained.

Jeans: Blue jeans are one of the largest clothing categories on Ebay, and fortunately for resellers, they are in abundance at thrift stores and garage sales. Check the crotches for rips, and make sure the inside labels are intact. Denim jeans are usually easy to list as many have the style and size (waist and inseam) on the label. As with most items, larger sizes tend to sell best, although high-end denim will usually sell despite the size.

Men's Hats: Vintage fedora and cowboy hats have always been quick and easy sales for me on Ebay, especially when they are leather or suede. Vintage snapback baseball and trucker hats are also good pieces to pick up.

Men's Flannel Shirts: Cotton men's flannel shirts are highly sought after on Ebay. The softer and thicker the material, the better they sell. Though the best-sellers are the vintage ones, any shirt, regardless of age, that has pearl snaps will typically sell the fastest.

Nylons: I have had great success selling new-in-the-package women's nylons, which I can usually find at Goodwill in an out-of-the-way bin. I also find hosiery at estate sales. Usually, I can find several packages in the same size at the thrift stores and estate sales. Unless they are vintage (vintage nylons can bring hundreds of dollars per pair!), I sell nylons in lots by size.

Overalls: Blue jean denim overalls are hard to find new in the stores, which is why they are popular with customers on Ebay. Maternity overalls are an incredibly hot seller. I have found that the brand does not matter when it comes to overalls. I pick up both full-length and short styles as well as overall dresses and skirts.

Puffer Coats & Vests: Outerwear in the "puffer" style (quilted and puffy) is always a good seller on Ebay for men, women, and children. However, note the size and weight before picking up puffer jackets as the larger ones will not fit into a Flat Rate Priority Mail padded mailer or box. They are still okay to buy to resell; just note that the shipping cost will be higher as they will have to go via regular Parcel or Priority.

Shoes & Boots: The secondhand shoe market on Ebay is enormous. Good, clean shoes from better-known brands can bring in good money. Familiarize yourself with the season's trends so you will know what to look for when sourcing. As with clothing, larger sizes of shoes tend to sell the fastest. High-end boots are also good sellers.

Sweaters: Well-made sweaters, especially those in cashmere, are in demand during the Fall and Winter on Ebay. While I do not live in an area where designer brands are sold, I can still find sweaters from Land's End, Eileen Fisher, and L.L. Bean that sell well online.

Vests: My Goodwill stores (there are three locations close to where I live) all have designated racks for vests. I always look through them, searching for designer brands and outerwear (as many times puffer vests are placed in with the vests rather than the coats). Vests with novelty patterns and prints are usually good sellers.

Vintage Tee Shirts: Tee shirts from the 1990s and before can be highly collectible. I look for concert and sports tees in good condition, although sought-after designs can sell regardless of condition.

Women's Shirts: After denim jackets, my favorite items to pick up at thrift stores and garage sales to resell are women's shirts and tops. They are often lightweight, making them easy to list and ship. As with all clothing, I focus on better brand names and larger sizes when sourcing shirts.

I deal primarily with men's and women's tops and outerwear. Since those are the categories of clothing that I am most familiar with, those are the pieces I am naturally drawn to when I am out at garage sales and thrift stores.

If you have kids, you may have a knack for children's clothing. If you love shoes, footwear may be just the item you hunt for. While I have shared the items that work best for my business model, please do not let that stop you from sourcing the styles you are most interested in. You will be much more successful reselling items you like versus picking up items you hate.

Sizes: When selling used clothing on Ebay, size matters, especially when dealing with more common brands. High-end designer clothing will sell in any size (and let's face it, most of the prominent brand-name designers only sell smaller sizes, anyway). However, mall store brands that are readily available everywhere tend to sell best on Ebay when they are in larger sizes.

In general, I stick to the "Small/Medium/Large" sizing, i.e., NOT specific fitted sizes such as "Size 4" or "Size 10." I find that someone is much more likely to buy a size "Large" shirt than a "Size 12" shirt. Most clothing sizes run differently according to the designer, too, so sticking to the "S/M/L" range is easier on me as a seller and for my buyers. I will be talking more about providing clothing measurements in your Ebay listings coming up.

I am always looking for larger clothing sizes, size "Extra Large" and up, for women. Women's plus sizes are typically marked as "0X, 1X, 2X, 3X, etc."; or with a "W," such as "22W" or "28W." Clothes labeled "XXL" and "XXXL" are usually considered to still fall under "regular sizing"; however, they are some of my best-selling sizes. Let's be honest: most women would prefer to buy a "regular size XXL" than a "plus size 1X" (even though in many brands, they are the same size).

Larger sizes are always the first to sell out new in the stores, so they are usually easy to resell on Ebay as they are in demand. Some people are also very self-conscious of their size and are embarrassed to shop in a brick-and-mortar store. So, they turn to Ebay to shop in private.

While I steer away from "Petite" women's clothing, I do pick up "Tall" sizes. Very few stores carry "Tall" sized women's clothing, so statuesque ladies must go online to find styles that will fit them. "Petite" sizes do sell; they just tend to sell more slowly for me, so I focus on items that I can move faster.

Men's large sizes are often the same as women's (i.e., "2XL, 3XL, 4XL"), although, with men's buttoned shirts, you do get into neck and sleeve markings. I love finding big and tall men's clothing, which is usually marked with a "T" (i.e., "XLT, 2LXT, XXXT"). Just as "Tall" sizing is a niche category in women's clothing, it is also a specialty size in men's and hard to find in the stores, meaning men must shop online for it. I will pick up a dress shirt from a lower-end brand if I find it in a "Tall."

However, as I have said, a high-end designer brand will usually sell despite the size. That is why it is important to look at the labels when sourcing clothing. A Gucci shirt will sell even if it is a size "Small" just because it is Gucci. Likewise, an Old Navy jacket in a "3X" will sell despite Old Navy being a common mall brand. I will pick up a Walmart brand if it is a size "4X" but won't even look twice at it if it's an "XL" or smaller. However, I will grab an "XXS" designer top if I see it.

Condition: Unless you are selling a hard-to-find, vintage, and/or extremely high-end designer brand of clothing, the piece's condition is critical when it comes to selling it on Ebay. It can be hard to give a piece of clothing a rigorous inspection in the middle of a crowded thrift store, but here are some things I make sure to look over before heading to check out:

Buttons: I look to make sure all buttons, including those on cuffs and pockets, are all intact. I pass on items that need new buttons as I do not have the time to find replacements. Note that if you find a high-end designer piece that is missing buttons, you can still buy the item and remove the remaining buttons to sell on their own if they are stamped with the designer's name.

Labels: A mistake I have made several times is buying an article of clothing that was missing a size label. I sometimes get so excited by spotting a brand name that I miss the fact that the original owner of the piece cut out the label with its size. While you can provide measurements for a piece of clothing with its label cut out, most buyers want the labels intact. Remember that not all size labels are on the inside collar; some are on the garment's inside body.

Pilling: Those little balls that form on your cotton shirts after they have been washed multiple times? It is called pilling, and it instantly screams that an item is in too worn of condition for resale. You can use a sweater shaver on these garments if the pilling is contained in one small area, especially if it's a valuable piece; but if the entire piece is covered in pilling, pass on it.

Pockets: Be sure to look at both the outside and inside pockets of garments (many trench coats, for example, have pockets in the lining) for rips. A bonus to checking pockets is that you might find some forgotten cash inside. Although, you also might find used tissues. Yuck!

Seams: I always give the seams a quick look to make sure there are no tears or rips. If you (or someone else in your house) can sew, minor tears along the seam can be repaired relatively easily. However, unless it is a high-end item, I do not want to waste my time doing any clothing repairs.

Stains: I always put back any item of clothing that has stains on it. While some stains can be treated and washed out, I do not have the time to deal with repairs.

Zippers: I make sure zippers are intact and functioning, i.e., not sticking. While there are zipper lubricants you can try on stuck zippers, I typically find that malfunctioning zippers are not worth dealing with unless they are vintage or designer pieces.

Washing & Drying: Should you wash clothes before listing them on Ebay? Some clothing sellers wash all items except those that are new with tags. Other sellers only steam clothing. And others list them as is.

Unless the item is dry clean only, I machine wash and tumble dry all clothing I sell on Ebay. Many other Ebay sellers do NOT wash the clothes they list, but I do for a few reasons.

Since I source most clothing from thrift stores, namely Goodwill, the pieces almost always have an odor. None of the thrift stores in my area wash the clothes they sell, so many still have the original owners' scent on them. Plus, they pick up the odors from all the other items they are bunched in with. There is a "thrift store" smell that you become familiar with if you shop at secondhand stores!

Some thrift stores, especially the Goodwill Outlets, spray the clothing they receive through donations to kill potential bed bugs. This chemical solution causes me to have an allergic reaction when I touch the garment; so, washing clothing from "The Bins" is especially crucial for me. Most resellers who source at the Goodwill Outlets do wash the clothing before listing it, unless, of course, it is new with tags.

If you wash a piece of clothing that still has the original tags attached, it will no longer be new with tags, and therefore the value will be decreased. I do not find too many new with tags clothing items, but when I do, I put them aside and list them as I found them.

I have had garments that reeked of perfume while others stunk of body odor. Throwing them into the wash is just an easy decision for me. Also, remember that just because you do not detect an odor does not mean that your buyer won't. I once sold a suede jacket that I had not washed because it was dry clean only and because it looked and smelled (to me) fine. However, the woman who bought it left me neutral feedback complaining that it reeked of perfume and that she had to have it professionally dry cleaned to get the smell out. Had I just disclosed in the listing that the item was unwashed, I could have saved myself the neutral feedback mark.

I use fragrance-free laundry detergent as well as non-scented dryer sheets for the clothes I list on Ebay. While I want to clean the items, I do not want to add any scent to them. Some buyers are sensitive to any smells; I have had buyers specifically request that I NOT use scented dryer sheets on items or put dryer sheets into packages (some sellers try to get away with not washing clothing by tucking a dryer sheet in them). I would also recommend NOT spraying clothing with Febreze or any other fabric spray as people can be sensitive to their fragrances. Even unscented products can adversely affect some customers.

For items that, for whatever reason, cannot be washed but have an odor, you can try leaving them outside to air out. Or you can place the item in the freezer, as the cold temperature typically kills the scent. I have used the freezer technique for vintage men's hats with a musty smell.

Freshly washed clothing is also just more pleasant for me to handle. Since I need to touch the clothes to photograph, measure, list, and then prepare for shipment, making sure they are clean makes the whole selling process much more enjoyable. After all, I do not want a pile of dirty, stinky clothes on my desk or on me!

Ironing: Since I sell a lot of shirts on Ebay, ironing is necessary. I picked up an ironing board at Goodwill for $4, and I use an iron I have owned for years. While clothing will get wrinkled when folded up to be shipped out, ironing out wrinkles makes garments look much better in the pictures. Ask yourself if you would buy a shirt if the picture showed it full of wrinkles before dismissing the idea of ironing clothing.

It is not just shirts I iron, however. Jacket collars are notoriously hard to get to lie down flat, but a quick press of the iron usually takes care of it. I also run into hems that have turned up, as well as cuffs, but ironing makes the fabric lie flat.

Steaming: In addition to an iron and ironing board, I also have a handheld steamer that I use when an item only has a few wrinkles. Note that many full-time clothing resellers invest in large, industrial steamers. The great thing about a commercial-grade garment steamer is that it gets out the wrinkles and sanitizes the item, meaning it does not need to be washed. A steamer is an investment, so I recommend waiting until you gain experience in reselling clothing before deciding if you want to splurge on one for your business.

Reliable Brands to Pick Up: There are tens of thousands of clothing labels out there; some are hot sellers, while some you cannot give away. High-end designer clothing in good condition will, of course, always sell. But if you are like me and do not live in an area where expensive clothing is worn or even sold, you can still find sellable clothing.

I live in Iowa, and the clothing brands I find secondhand are from your typical mall stores. Yet, I have successfully added clothes to my inventory by looking for unique pieces in excellent condition. I would guess that you will find the brands listed below as well, which means you will be on your way to making money by reselling them on Ebay!

Another benefit of being restricted to run-of-the-mill brands is that I do not have to worry about counterfeit clothing. I highly doubt anyone is making knock-off Old Navy coats the way they produce fake Gucci purses!

Here are just some of the brand names that I have personally sourced here in Iowa and have sold on Ebay:

- American Eagle
- Anne Klein

- Ann Taylor and Ann Taylor LOFT
- Banana Republic
- Cabela's
- CABI
- Carhartt
- Calvin Klein
- Chico's
- CJ Banks
- Columbia
- Disney
- Duluth Trading Company
- Eddie Bauer
- Eileen Fisher
- Express
- Free People
- Gap
- Harley Davidson
- J. Crew
- J. Jill
- Land's End
- Lane Bryant
- Levi's
- Life Is Good
- L.L. Bean
- Lucky Brand
- Nike
- Patagonia
- Ralph Lauren
- Talbots
- Tommy Bahama
- Tommy Hilfiger
- Torrid
- Victoria's Secret & PINK

Again, please remember that these are the brands I have personally been able to find in my area and have successfully sold on

Ebay. You may be in an area that sells higher-end designer pieces, meaning you will have a better chance of finding more expensive clothing at your thrift stores.

Also, as I discussed earlier, size, style, and condition are crucial factors when sourcing clothing to resell. You likely will not have much luck selling a size small white tee shirt from Express that shows wear, but you will likely be able to sell a size large sparkly dress from Express that is in excellent condition.

Storing & Organizing Clothing Inventory: When you sell on Ebay, you tend to accumulate a lot of stuff, but inventory usually takes up the most space. This is true whether you sell books, collectibles, or clothing. The one downside of clothing is that while one piece is relatively lightweight, a bunch of it together is heavy. I have broken several clothing racks over the years when I overloaded them with clothes.

I finally invested in industrial clothing racks that I found on Amazon. You can find sturdy ones (I recommend a rack that holds at least 250-pounds) for around $60 online. Make sure to get a rack with rollers so that you can easily move it around. I have six of these industrial racks for hanging clothing.

However, if you do not want to invest in clothing, there are other ways to store clothes. Many full-time clothing resellers store their inventory in plastic bins. Once they have listed the item on Ebay, they fold it and seal it in a clear poly bag. They then label the bag with the contents (some just write this on a piece of tape while others print out an inventory label) and store it in the bin. The bins themselves are labeled, making the item easy to find once it sells.

How To List Clothing on Ebay: Too many people focus only on obtaining items to sell online and neglect the other essential parts of selling on Ebay, especially getting the item listed for sale. A good listing makes all the difference in how fast your item will sell and how much and how happy the customer will be once they receive their order.

Clothing is tricky for several reasons. Some pieces may look like they are for a man but are sized for a woman. There are hundreds of categories and sub-categories to list clothing in. A "Small" in one brand may be a "Medium" in another. Some people take measurements one way, while you may take them differently.

It is very easy to make a mistake when listing a piece of clothing, resulting in an unhappy customer, a return, and possibly negative feedback. However, taking the time to list clothes properly will help cut down on any issues.

Men's vs. Women's Clothing: The first thing you need to do before you list an item of clothing on Ebay is to determine whether it is for a man or a woman. I know you are probably thinking (or saying), "DUH! Of course, you will know if an item is for a man or a woman!" However, unless an item is marked on the label as being sized explicitly by gender, it can sometimes be hard to tell who the garment was made for, especially when dealing with shirts and coats.

Fortunately, it is usually easy to determine whether a piece is for a male or a female, and that is by looking at the way the item is buttoned or zippered. The buttons are on the right-hand side for men's buttoned shirts, and the buttonholes are on the left. It is the opposite for women's buttoned shirts: the buttons are on the left-hand side, and the buttonholes are on the right.

For coats and jackets, the zipper pull tab is usually on the right-hand side for men and the left-hand side for women. When listing a zippered jacket on Ebay, I often must double-check my own jackets to see which side the zipper is on!

If the buttons and/or zippers still are not clearing the issue of gender up for you, look at the piece's silhouette. Women's shirts and jackets tend to be tapered a bit at the waist. Also, check the measurements. A men's "medium" will measure larger than a women's will.

Of course, in today's world, there are those items that are unisex. While a lot of unisex pieces are marked as such, not all are. I have had clothes that looked like they were for women but were sized for men. In these instances, I list the item as "unisex" and make it clear in the listing that the customer needs to thoroughly review the measurements I have provided before buying the piece.

Clothing Categories: The first thing you need to decide when creating your Ebay listing for an article of clothing is what category to put it in. Clothing accounts for a considerable portion of the listings on Ebay's website, and there are lots of choices on how to categorize your item. Is the jacket you have a windbreaker or a parka? Is the men's shirt you are listing a dress shirt or a casual one?

I always do a completed listing search of all items I list on Ebay, whether it is a vintage collectible or an article of clothing. Not only does this enable me to see what the going price is (more about pricing clothing coming up), but I can also see what category other sellers are putting the same item in.

While the first category you list an item in is free, you can list that same item in a second category for an additional fee. However, I strongly advise saving yourself the fees and only listing your items in one category each. If you have a keyword-loaded title and have filled out the correct item specifics, customers should find your items no matter what category you have them listed under.

Writing A Great Title: A good, keyword-loaded title is essential for selling anything on Ebay, including clothing. When listing an item of clothing, I include the brand, color, size, pattern, and anything else I can cram into the available title space. Remember that with an Ebay title, you do not need to write a proper sentence but rather fill up space with keywords that will bring in the most traffic.

It is not enough to type in "Green Ralph Lauren Shirt." A better title would be "Mens Green RALPH LAUREN Polo Shirt EXTRA LARGE Pony Cotton EUC." Notice how I only capitalized a few words; you do not want to type anything in all capitals as it comes across as yelling. I also added in "EUC," which means "Excellent Used Condition."

Misspellings are common in Ebay titles, so it is essential to double-check that you have correctly spelled the clothing item's brand name. You do not want to miss a sale because you left an "I" out of Tommy Hilfiger.

Another tip for writing any Ebay title, including one for clothing, is to put both spellings of a word in. I often include both "grey" and "gray" in the title because people spell that color differently.

Do not clutter up your title with pointless words such as "LOOK!" Also, avoid any punctuation marks as they not only take up valuable space, but they can also mess up search results. I always type "Mens," not "Men's" in my titles, for instance.

Accurately Describing Condition: After the title comes the condition field. Ebay allows you to choose one of four condition choices for clothing:

- **New with Tags**
- **New without Tags**
- **New with Defects**
- **Pre-Owned**

Because I buy most of the clothing I resell at estate sales and Goodwill, almost all of what I sell on Ebay is *Pre-Owned.* I only list an item as *New with Tags* if it, in fact, still has the original price tags attached.

I rarely use the *New without Tags* or *New with Defects* options. The only time I list an item as *New without Tags* is if it came from my own closet, and I can guarantee it was never washed or worn (washing an article of clothing automatically makes it a second-hand piece). Otherwise, to ensure I am not misleading customers, I classify clothing without tags as *Pre-Owned*.

Technically, an item is *Pre-owned* once the original buyer purchased it, regardless of whether the piece was ever worn or even washed. So even if you buy an item at a thrift store that still has the original tags attached, it is still, to some people, considered to be *Pre-Owned*, although very few resellers will classify it as such.

Since I rarely find *New with Tags* clothing at thrift stores to resell on Ebay, this is not usually an issue for me. However, even when I find clothing with the original tags still attached, I sometimes still list them as *Pre-Owned* if the tags are torn or damaged in any way. Customers expect *New with Tags* items to look like they just came off the original store rack.

Under the condition field is a section where you can **Highlight any defects, missing parts, scratches, or wear and tear.** It is important to be very thorough here and disclose all issues, no matter how small they may be. Filling out this section offers you as the seller a level of protection from a buyer coming back after the sale to claim you did not correctly describe the item. I include any flaws in this area, and I put the same information into the actual item description, too.

Photos: I have sold clothing on Ebay for years and never used a mannequin for many of those years. While I have since added a mannequin to my photography space, I only use it for items that look significantly better on one. Otherwise, I just hang my items against a flat surface for photos. If you plan to make clothing the main part of your inventory or even a large part of it, then investing in a mannequin to take photos of clothing is a good idea. There are many options available on Ebay where you can find a good mannequin for around $50.

However, if you are only planning to sell clothes occasionally, or if you do not have a lot of extra room to set up a mannequin, do not fret as there are ways to photograph clothing without one. For years, I took clothing photos hanging from a hook on the back of my bedroom door. I have since "upgraded" to hanging them on a hook on a white wall to give the items a clean background.

While clothing usually does look best on a mannequin, I prefer the ease of hanging clothes against a white wall. Some resellers invest in professional photo backdrops and expensive lighting, but I get by with my white wall next to a large window, which gives me a lot of natural light. Whether you use electric lights or the sunlight, you want to make sure the item's actual color comes through in the pictures and small details such as the fabric's texture and the details on the buttons.

Ebay allows you to add up to twelve photos to each listing, and I advise taking advantage of that number by providing as many pictures as possible. Take photos from the front, back, and sides of each item you are listing. Zoom in on any unique details. Take pictures of the labels, the size label on the collar, and the fabric label, usually found along the tops and jackets inside. If there are any flaws on the item, even very tiny ones, take photos of them. Clothing with flaws can still sell if you are upfront and honest about its issues. Give your customers the feeling that they are holding the item in person, turning it over in their hands as they would if they were shopping in a brick-and-mortar store.

If you are unsure how to take pictures of clothing best, look around at other Ebay listings to compare how different sellers present their items. While you do not want to copy someone else's photo style outright, you do want to take note of which listings appeal to you as a shopper. Do you prefer clothing on mannequins? Do you like how clothes look hung up? What DON'T you like about some of the pictures you see? Use these impressions to guide you in your own photographing of clothing.

One thing that you may see other sellers doing is putting props in their pictures, such as flowers or even accessories. While this may be visually appealing, it can distract from the item you are trying to sell, and if you are adding jewelry and shoes in a picture of a sweater, buyers may assume they are BUYING everything in the photo. Online shoppers are notorious for purchasing simply based on the pictures and failing to read the actual listing. Avoid any confusion and possible customer backlash by ONLY showing the item for sale in your pictures.

Item Specifics: Depending on what category you are listing in on Ebay, various clothing-specific fields will be available for you to select from. Providing as many details as possible on each piece of clothing will help sell it faster and will also cut down on customer questions or complaints.

Usually, these fields are for **Brand, Style, Size Type and Size, Color, Pattern, Material,** and **Country of Origin**. If you are unsure about the style, look at the completed listings to see what other sellers have categorized it as. Brand, size, material, and country of origin should all be described on the garment label.

For certain items, such as men's dress shirts, you will also see fields for the collar and cuff type. Listings for pants will include size fields for the rise and inseam. While you will end up still wanting to type all these details into your description, you still want to fill out this section as it is what buyers use to narrow down the search results.

In late 2019, Ebay implemented a massive overhaul of their

item-specific fields, most of them in the clothing categories. Now there are two distinct sections under **Item Specifics: Required** and **Suggested.** You MUST fill out all the *Required* fields, and you SHOULD fill out as many of the *Suggested* as possible. All fields will help buyers find your item among the millions of other Ebay listings.

When filling out the item-specific fields, try to choose the options provided in the drop-down menus over typing in your information. The choices already in Ebay's system are the ones that appear to buyers when they are searching the site. Entering in your own specifics will result in your item being excluded from that section's particular search. When in doubt, it is better to leave an item-specific field blank than writing in your own term.

Writing A Great Description: After you have chosen a category, written a title, uploaded your photos, and selected the item specifics, it is time to write the description for the piece of clothing you are selling. While it is tempting just to list the facts, such as only the brand and size, taking a few extra moments to write a great description will help sell your item faster and cut down on customer questions or problems.

Because the clothing market on Ebay is so crowded, it is important to make YOUR listing stand out from the rest. I always start by stating what the item is in bold fonts, such as "Mens Red Gap Puffer Vest." Under that, I try to really "sell" the item by writing something like, "This stylish red vest will keep you warm all winter long!" As you can see, I do not write an entire advertisement for the piece, but I do add a little extra to the listing to catch potential buyers' eyes.

After my title and "sales pitch," I then follow up with all the information I can give the buyer, including: fabric (look on the label and copy down what is there), washing instructions, any zippers or buttons, pockets, and of course the size and measurements (more on taking measurements coming up). Whatever details you chose in the item specifics section should be repeated in your description. If I have washed the item, I always include "Comes to you freshly washed!" Finally, I provide the condition of the piece.

Providing an accurate statement of the condition for anything, especially a piece of clothing, is tricky. What may look to be brand new to you could appear worn to a customer. As with all items I sell on Ebay, I tend to understate the condition. If a piece is in excellent condition, I describe it as great. Instead of saying an item is in very good condition, I will state that it is merely in good condition.

If an item still has the original price tag on it, I do state that it is brand new. If the original hang tags were cut off, it immediately makes the item pre-owned. Washed but never worn also means pre-owned. If I purchased the item at an estate sale and know for a fact the owner did not smoke, I will state, "From a clean, smoke-free home!"

Clothing Measurements: If you want to sell clothing successfully on Ebay, you will have to take measurements. A size "large" in one brand may fit like a "small" in another. If you only list what the label says, you will be inundated with questions asking you what the measurements are, so you might as well take them to start with.

While it may sound tedious, taking measurements is relatively easy to do. There are many ways to take measurements, though; here is how I take them:

I provide three measurements for shirts and coats: Across the Chest, Sleeve, and **Body Length.** As I mentioned earlier, I put an explanation of how I take these measurements in my listings.

To get the **Across the Chest measurement**, I lay the item out on a flat surface and place the tape measure starting under the armpit on one side and then stretch the measurer out to the other armpit. I provide that number in my listings, although doubling the number is also an option as those give the buyer the chest size.

For the **Sleeve measurement**, I place the tape measure at the seam near the shoulder and stretch it down to the cuff. Another option is to measure from the top of the sleeve near the collar and down to the cuff.

For the **Length measurement**, I place the tape measure at the top of the piece at the seam next to the collar (but not including the collar) and bring it down to the longest part of the garment's hem.

It is also important to note if an item, say a women's shirt, is cinched in the waist. If it is, providing the waist measurement is helpful. Some customers will also ask for the shoulder size, meaning the width from one shoulder to the next. You will want to provide the hip measurements for garments that fall below the hip, such as trench coats. I take the waist, shoulder, and hip measurements just as I do across the chest by laying the item flat and measuring the width.

For pants, shorts, or skirts, I provide measurements for the **waist, hips** (measuring across the widest part), **inseam** (length from crotch to hem or cuff), **front rise** (length from waistline to crotch), **rear rise** (length from waistline to crotch in the back), and the **length from the waistline to the hem.**

Fortunately, many pants include the waist and inseam measurement on the label, but some buyers still want the actual measurements. For pants with the label measurements, you can always try listing them without additional measurements if you are open to providing exact measurements for those who ask.

I try to be proactive when listing and provide as much information as possible the first time. Otherwise, someone will inevitably ask for a measurement, meaning I will have to go into my inventory room to pull the item to measure it. However, some sellers will tell the customer that the only measurements they can provide are the ones they have already included in the listing, even if that is only what is on the garment label.

I measure across the chest, across the waist, and the length from the waist to the hem for dresses. If there is no waist seam, I measure the length from the collar seam back to the dress hem.

I sometimes sell accessories such as hats, neckties, purses, and shoes, in addition to clothing. For neckties, I measure the width at the widest point. For hats, I look for a label inside indicating the size. If there is not one, I measure the inside diameter. Customers shopping for purses want to know the width, height, depth, and handle drop, which is the distance from the top of the handle or strap to the top of the bag. Finally, when selling shoes, I include the size on the label as well as heel height and width.

Again, while taking all these measurements may seem like overkill, providing them will not only help you sell the item faster, but it will cut down on customer questions. You are also protecting yourself from a buyer coming back and claiming an item was not the size you stated in the listing.

Shipping Clothing: A significant factor in pricing clothing is whether to offer "free" shipping. I put "free" in parenthesis because nothing is ever truly free; to offer "free" shipping, I must add the cost of postage to the item's price. Therefore, I must know what the shipping cost will be before I list an item on Ebay.

As I have mentioned several times, clothing is a massive category on Ebay, and the competition is fierce. I am a Power Seller and a Top-Rated Seller, so my listings are supposed to be the first in searches. However, with so many other people selling clothing, it is easy for even a seller like me to find their clothing listings buried amongst all the others.

Offering "free" shipping is one way to bring your clothing listings to the top of the Ebay search results. Most of the clothing I sell can ship via *First Class* or fit into a *USPS Priority Flat Rate Bubble Mailer*. For those items, I will usually offer "free" shipping. However, I do charge the customer shipping for bulky, heavy pieces.

I always give my customers two shipping choices on clothing, the first being the economy choices of *Parcel Select* for packages weighing over 16-ounces or *First Class* if the item weighs under 16-ounces. I then also offer the optional choice of expedited shipping via *Priority Mail*, which they can choose to pay for. I also ship through Ebay's Global Shipping program, and all international customers pay shipping.

Most clothing you sell on Ebay will ship via either First Class Mail, Parcel Select, or Priority Mail. *First Class Mail* is the service you use when you send a letter. One stamp equals one ounce for letters but note that it costs more for larger, thicker envelopes that most Ebay shipments will go in. You can ship up to 16-ounces (one pound) via *First Class*. Shipping items via *First Class* is where having a digital postal scale comes in handy as you can get your package down to the exact ounce. Every ounce means more money spent, so it is essential to get as close of a weight on your item as possible.

However, even with a digital scale, finding the exact ounce can be challenging as you need an item's weight before you list an item. I weigh all items WITH an envelope or box to get a general weight. It does not have to be the exact envelope or box that I will eventually use to ship the item in, but it gives me a general weight to go on as the shipping container alone can add up to over one pound to the weight of a package.

My trick is to add 3-ounces to the package's weight to account for packing materials. If I have a small item that, when placed in an envelope, weighs 5-ounces, I will list it as 8-ounces. That way, when it is in an envelope with a packing slip, I avoid the risk of the Post Office sending it back for insufficient postage.

I ship all clothing weighing under 16-ounces in plain poly mailer bags that I order online from Amazon, Ebay, ValueMailers, and Uline. Most tee shirts and men's dress shirts are light enough to be mailed via *First Class*, meaning I only need to add about $4 into the asking price to cover postage. If I have a shirt that I think is worth $10, I may price it at $14.99 with free *First-Class* shipping to cover the postage cost. Even though the shirt is priced slightly higher, it will show up high in the Ebay search results. Since some customers specifically search Ebay for free shipping items, offering the free shipping option is sometimes the only way customers will find your item.

And here is a tip that will save you when you create your next clothing listing: Instead of starting from scratch every time you need to create a new listing, open a listing that is currently live and click on the **Sell Similar** option. Then you can just change all the item specifics, including the shipping options and weight. This makes your listing time fly by as you do not have to go in and set up the *Calculated Shipping* option every time you list a new item!

It is crucial that whatever you sell on Ebay, especially clothing, is CLEAN and from SMOKE-FREE HOMES. If you are a smoker, be sure to keep your inventory and your packing supplies in an area away from the smoke. If your buyer detects even the slightest scent of cigarettes, they WILL complain.

Even though clothing isn't breakable, we still take the time to package it carefully for shipment. We wrap garments in packing paper before sliding them into their envelopes or boxes. If there is space between the wrapped piece of clothing and the box, we will add a bit more packing paper to prevent the item from bouncing around during transit.

One tip to make getting clothing into the *Priority Mail Flat Rate Bubble Mailer* is to put it into a small plain polybag, which then slides easily into the bubble mailer. This is especially helpful in shrinking down puffy coats and thick shirts to fit into the envelope.

Be sure to use plenty of packing tape, especially if you have a stuffed-to-the-brim bubble mailer. The last thing you want is the envelope busting open during shipment.

There is a reason you see so many resellers posting on social media about selling clothing. It is easy to find, relatively cheap to buy, easy to list and store, and easy to ship. Even if you do not want to make reselling clothing your full-time business, it is still worth taking the time to learn about how to flip clothes for profit on Ebay!

CHAPTER SIX:

TAKING EBAY PHOTOS

Sourcing items to sell is the most fun part of selling on Ebay. However, it is the nitty-gritty work of photographing and listing the items you are selling that will consume most of your time as a reseller.

Before you can list your items for sale on Ebay, you need to photograph them. Having good, clear photos of your items is essential in not only attracting customers but in getting top dollar.

I used to use a digital camera that I'd had for nearly ten years to take all my Ebay pictures, but I have exclusively used my iPhone for photos for the past several years. Today's smartphones are just as good, if not better, than many digital cameras, and taking pictures on your phone means you can upload them directly to Ebay through their app.

Whether you use a digital camera or smartphone, the most important thing is that the pictures are clear, not blurry, well-lit, and show the item's actual color, and that photos are cropped so that there is not a bunch of white space around them. You want the item itself to be front and center.

A common mistake I see new sellers make is taking photos of

their items on the floor or a cluttered counter. You do not want any other part of your home showing in the photo, just the item. Would you want to buy something you know has been on someone else's floor or near their dirty sink? Or worse, with someone's dirty, ragged fingernail in the shot?

An easy, cheap photo background involves taking two pieces of foam board (I buy mine at Dollar Tree for $1 each) and placing them together at a 90-degree angle (one laying on the table and then one propped up against the wall). This gives you a clean, white background both under and behind the photo. I have used this system for nearly a decade.

As I discussed in the previous chapter, if you are selling clothing, hang the garment up on the back of a door or against a white wall or on a mannequin against a solid color wall. While a white backdrop is preferable, a clean, solid wood color will do if you do not have one. Ensure all the wrinkles are ironed out, the buttons all buttoned, and the piece is lying flat against the door or wall. If you decide you want to become a full-time Ebay clothing seller, you can invest in a mannequin; but to start, the door or wall methods are just fine.

Whatever the item is that you are photographing, you will want to take a lot of pictures of it from all angles. When people shop in a brick-and-mortar store, they touch the items they are interested in and turn them over in their hands. You want to give your Ebay customers the same feeling when they are looking at your listings. When I photograph a coffee mug, for instance, I take a picture of each of the four sides and the top looking down into the mug and of the bottom.

When looking at multiple completed listings of items that have ended, the number one difference between ones that have sold and ones that have not is the photos. Great photos go a long way towards selling items on Ebay, so take the time to get yours right!

Item Pictures: Ebay allows sellers to add up to twelve photos per listing, and you should take full advantage of that and provide as many pictures as possible of the item you are selling. Take photos of the piece from every single angle, including from the top and the bottom. You want to give your customers the feeling they would have if they were in a brick-and-mortar store handling an item. You likely do not purchase something by only glancing at it briefly on the shelf, so you will sell more on Ebay if you give your customers pictures of your items from every angle.

For instance, if you are selling a coffee mug, take pictures of the front, back, both sides, bottom, along with a shot of the inside (customers want to see if there are any "spoon marks," i.e., scratches or discoloration). For clothes, take full-length shots of the garment's front and back and up-close pictures of hems, cuffs, pockets, and labels. If your item is battery-powered, take a photo of the open battery compartment to show that there is not any erosion. When I list vintage books, I take photos of the front and back cover, the spine, the first couple of title pages, and two to three photos of the text pages.

You want the item you are selling to be front and center in all pictures, so take the time to edit your photos to eliminate as much white space as possible. Ebay recently added the ability to remove your photo's background and turn the space to pure white. However, this is a new feature and has proven not to work very well with most items, sometimes cutting entire parts of the item itself out.

I do not worry about my pictures looking perfect; I focus on making sure my photo area is well lit and against a white background (such as a wall or piece of posterboard). I worry more about making sure my pictures are clear with the item in focus than I do the background.

When I take pictures of items to list on Ebay, I make sure to take up-close photos of any condition issues such as minor wear or damage. I disclose any faults in the listing, and I also direct buyers to look closely at the photos provided so they know exactly what they are buying. It is rare to find secondhand items that do not have even a tiny bit of wear and tear.

Still, by disclosing all issues and providing photos, you will not only have a better chance of the item selling, but you will also protect yourself from a customer complaining they received something that was not as described. Buyers understand that they are purchasing pre-owned items and do not expect them to be perfect, but they rightly expect that the seller provides them with an accurate condition.

It is important to take up-close pictures of details such as the maker's marks on ceramics, clothing labels (both the size label by the collar as well as fabric labels that may be located elsewhere, such as near the inside hem), and any inscriptions, as well as any condition issues. The cameras on most of today's smartphones take pictures that are just as good and sometimes even better than actual digital cameras. In particular, my iPhone is much better at capturing up-close details than the digital camera I used to use ever was.

After taking my pictures on my iPhone and editing them in my camera roll, I open the Ebay app, click on one of my active listings, and then click on the *Sell Similar* option. Ebay automatically asks if I want to keep or remove the photos from that listing; I select "remove" and then upload the photos I just took directly from my camera roll. I then save that listing as a *Draft* and switched over to my laptop to complete the listing.

Some Ebay sellers complete the entire listing process on their smartphones via the Ebay app; I just personally find it easier to finish listings on my computer, mainly because I sell so many different items with different shipping weights.

Note that you want the item's main photo, the one that will appear as the **Thumbnail** in the Ebay search results, to be the photo that shows your entire item. For instance, if you are selling a coffee mug, you want the mug's front to be the main thumbnail picture. Sometimes when I upload my photos from my phone into an Ebay listing, the photos upload out of order. This is yet another reason I like to finish listings on my computer, as it is easier to correct such details.

Ensure all photos are upright, not sideways or upside down, and do not upload blurry photos. I cannot tell you how many lousy item photos I see on Ebay, and poor-quality pictures can make it next to impossible for an item to sell. It is better to retake photos than upload poor ones.

Lighting: You do not need a fancy photography set-up to take Ebay photos, just a space with a lot of light. Good lighting is essential to taking clear pictures that capture color and detail, along with any flaws.

If your home or workspace is dark, you can easily brighten things up with lamps. If you frequently list many items online, you may want to invest in some professional lighting, such as a **ring lamp,** although I never found this necessary.

However, if you mainly list items in a similar category, such as clothing, you may find a professional lighting setup to be beneficial. If you rely on natural light for your photos, a lighting setup will allow you to list even on gloomy days. Ring light systems can be purchased online for as little as $50.

A **lightbox** is a tool that sellers of small items such as jewelry and miniatures like to use. Portable lightboxes can be purchased for around $50 online, although there are all sorts of YouTube tutorials on making your own using cardboard boxes and lights.

I take my Ebay photos in a room with lots of windows that provide ample natural lighting. I also turn on all the room's lights and a lamp to add more brightness. I want to make sure to capture the actual color and texture of the items I am selling. Rarely do I use my camera flash, which often distorts the product's actual color, making it appear lighter than it is. My iPhone has some editing features for the light that I occasionally use, especially if an item's color does not show up correctly (this usually happens to me with anything green).

Backdrops: I see many Ebay sellers who take pictures of items on their dirty carpet or with their messy kitchen in the background. I have even seen pictures of packaged food products taken on the floor with a pet's tail in the shot!

Taking pictures against a white background will work for most items, whether it is a white wall, a sheet, or a table. I have a straightforward setup of white poster boards for my photos. I set one on a table and the other against a wall to form a slight angle. I buy the boards at the dollar store for $1 each, and I also have a set in black for light-colored items that do not show up against a white background.

For larger items, it is easy to take pictures against a white wall. If you do not have a white wall, draping a white sheet from the ceiling can provide a nice backdrop. I have a blank, white wall in my office with a single nail that I hang clothes from to take photos. You want to make sure that whatever backdrop you use is clean and pattern-free so that nothing takes away from the item itself.

Whatever you use as your backdrop, just make sure that the item you are selling is the only item in the picture. I cannot tell you how many photos I see where other things and even people and pets are in the photos. Make sure to edit your hands/fingers out of pictures. I occasionally need to hold down a book page to get a photo, but I always edit my hand out. Unless you are a hand model, no one wants to see your chipped nails and cracked cuticles. Yuck!

Stock Photos: If you sell an item with a bar code in Ebay's catalog, a stock photo will often pop up to use as the main picture in your listing. And while many sellers use these photos, I do not like them, preferring to use my pictures. Sometimes I use Ebay's provided stock photo, but not as the main picture; I keep it in the listing and have it at the end of my photo lineup.

Stock photos indicate the item is brand new, and even if you have a new, unused item to sell, you likely picked it up secondhand. There may be differences in the item you are selling versus the product's original stock photo, including slight damage. And unless an item is brand new and in Ebay's catalog with the photo they provide or you have obtained permission from the manufacturer, wholesale, or liquidation company that the item came from to use their photos, it is unethical to use stock photos.

In some cases, it is even illegal to use a company's stock photo without their permission. If you are purchasing items via wholesale or liquidation and those companies provide you with stock photos, you will still need permission to use those pictures on Ebay. Do not go directly to a company's website and copy their pictures for your Ebay listing; not only will that get you into trouble with Ebay, but it could also result in legal action from the business whose photos you stole.

Even if the item I am selling matches the approved stock pictures exactly, I still take my own photos as I feel they best represent my specific products. While customers turn to Amazon to buy brand new items, they often come to Ebay looking for gently used products or extreme deals. So, while it is reasonable to expect an Amazon listing with an available quantity of one hundred products to use stock photos, on Ebay, most people are just selling one single version of each of the items they have listed. And by providing photos of the exact item you are selling, you assure customers that what they see in the picture is exactly what they are getting.

While you will likely see other sellers using stock photos on Ebay, please remember that just because some people are getting away with it does not mean you should, too. Do you really want to risk losing your Ebay account because you didn't want to take a few pictures? I know I don't!

CHAPTER SEVEN:

CREATING EBAY LISTINGS

The first Ebay listing you create is the most labor-intensive one as you will have to fill out all the various fields, including all the shipping options. However, once you have created your first listing, the second listing and all those that follow will be much easier as you can select the Sell Similar option, which will copy the information from the first listing into the second, meaning you will only have to change specific fields, not start entirely from scratch. I will discuss that more after I walk you through creating your first listing.

If you are creating your first-ever listing, first **log into your Ebay account**, and click on the **Sell** tab at the very top of the page on the left-hand side. Even if you have already been on the site earlier, you usually will have to log in again; don't worry, this is just an added level of Ebay security so that they are assured that it is indeed you logging into your account. Ebay has a lot of protections built into their site, so get used to having to re-log into your account frequently

If you have already listed something for sale on Ebay, instead of clicking on the *Sell* tab, you will go to your **Seller Hub** and click on the **Create listing** button, which will give you two options: **single listing** or **multiple quantity listing**. Choose the single listing option.

You will then be taken to a new screen titled **Tell us what you're selling**. Here you can enter a UPC, ISBN, ePID, part number, product name, or general description of your item. For this example, let's use "Ralph Lauren men's shirt." Ebay will then show you several options, including if they already have the item you sell in their product catalog. If you picked up this shirt at a thrift store, you will be listing it secondhand and not using Ebay's product catalog. So, you will click **Continue without selecting a product**.

Ebay will now bring up their **Create your listing** page for you, which is a page you will become very familiar with as you create your listings. The first section of the listing page is **Listing details**.

The first field you will need to fill out is for the **Title**. A great title is key to selling your item, as it will help buyers find your listing. You want to use all the 80-character spaces allowed, even if it does not read like a proper sentence or headline. "Red Men's Shirt" is a lousy title as it will be drowned out in the search against all the other red shirts listed. However, "XL Red Blue Plaid Mens Ralph Lauren Button-Down Shirt Long Sleeve Thick Cotton" not only tells the customer exactly what the item is but it is loaded with keywords to make finding the listing in the search much easier.

There is no need to check the box to make your title bold or enter a subtitle; these are just added features for which Ebay charges you extra fees. In all my years of selling on Ebay, I have never once paid for these options.

After filling in the title area, you will need to select a **Category** for your item, which is another way for buyers to narrow down their search. Let's stick with the Ralph Lauren shirt. Obviously, since this is a clothing piece, you will want to select the

"Clothing, Shoes & Accessories" category. You will then be able to narrow down the category even further by selecting "Men's Clothing" and then "Casual Shirts." Ebay gives you the option of selecting a second category for an extra charge, but one category is plenty.

If you have an Ebay Store subscription, you will also choose your **Store Categories,** which you can set up when creating your Ebay Store. Some sellers do not have any store categories, while others break their items down into very specific sections.

To set up your store's categories, click on the **Marketing** tab at the top of your **My Ebay page** and select **Store**. Then click on the **Manage My Store** icon in the top right-hand corner of your store's front page. Under the **Store Management** section on the left-hand side, select **Store Categories** under **Store Design** to access the **Manage Store Categories** section.

Once you have chosen your Ebay category and store categories (if applicable), **Condition** is the next field you will encounter. Representing your item's correct condition is very important as buyers can file a claim with Ebay and get their money back if you say an item is new but is used, or if it is in worse condition than you state. Legally, once you take an item out of a store, it is classified as secondhand, so even if it still has the tags and has never been worn, it is technically used. However, new in the box or new with tag items are almost always listed as "new" by Ebay sellers.

Depending on the category, there may be more choices than just new or used. For instance, there are four in the clothing category: *New with Tags, New without Tags, New with Defects,* and *Pre-Owned.* If that Ralph Lauren shirt has been washed but never worn, you need to list it as pre-owned.

There is also a **Condition description** field for you to write in any specific information you want the customer to know about.

Be sure to disclose even the tiniest of issues. Flawed items can still sell, but you want to make sure you detail all missing parts, stains, rips, or cracks an item may have.

One of the best pieces of advice I ever got for selling on Ebay was to under-promise and over-deliver. I often understate the condition of my items. If an item is in like-new condition, I say it is in "very good condition." If it is in good condition, I will say it is "fair." Not only is condition highly debatable among buyers, but when a customer gets something in better shape than they thought it would be, they are always pleased. My feedback reflects this as several of my customers write, "Better condition than expected!"

The next step in the listing process is to upload the **Photos** of your item. Ebay allows up to twelve pictures per listing; take advantage of that by uploading lots of photos. As we discussed earlier, good, clear pictures will help sell your item for top dollar.

I upload my photos from my phone directly to Ebay, and I do this in one of two ways. The first way is to skip inserting the pictures while creating the listing on my computer, saving the listing as a draft, switching to the Ebay app on my phone, opening the draft, and uploading the photos.

Or I have a second way where I create a draft first on my phone by clicking on the Sell Similar option on one of my active listings. When I do this, a new listing is created. I delete the photos, add in the new pictures, and save the listing as a draft. I then switch back to my computer to complete the listing.

I know this probably sounds very involved and complicated, but trust me when I say that once you have done this process a few times, it takes less than 30 seconds to complete going forward.

But, back to creating your listing:

Next comes the **Item Specifics** fields. Again, depending on what category you are listing in, there could be a lot or only a couple of options. Only the fields with **red asterisk stars** next to them are mandatory; these are all under the **Required** section. The section underneath is **Recommended.** While it can be daunting to fill out all the item-specific options available, it is best to choose as many as possible to help potential buyers find your item on Ebay's site.

The following section to fill out is **Item description**, which is where you really get to "sell" your item. Put in as much information as you can think of; the more details you give, the more likely you are to sell your item, plus it will drastically cut down on questions from potential buyers.

For instance, when listing a book, I type in everything that is on the cover page, including the publishing house. I also measure the book. You would not believe how many questions I get when I do not put in the measurements!

While all these details may seem like a waste of time for you, remember that you are competing with thousands of other listings, especially if you are selling a popular item such as a current toy or video game. Let your buyers know the REAL condition of the item, and if it comes from a smoke-free home, mention that, too.

Once you have filled out the item description section, it is time for **Selling details**, which is where you will decide the **Format**, whether to list your item at **Auction-style** OR **Fixed Price**. This is where research comes into play. If you have done a completed listing search on an item and found out it has been selling at a consistent price, then set yours the same at *Fixed Price.* If prices are all over the place, price yours somewhere in the middle. Or, you can take a risk and start an auction.

While Ebay used to be known solely for auctions, most experienced sellers list their items at *Fixed Price* these days. Most buyers who shop on Ebay now expect items to be at *Fixed Price*, so auctions tend to get overlooked.

I only put my items up for auction if I cannot find any completed listings for them and have no idea what to price them as, or if I am looking to move inventory and decide to try auctions to quickly sell some things and to generate traffic to my other listings. Mostly, though, I stick to *Fixed Price* listings to set the price I want.

As a new seller, I would try a few items at auction starting at 99-cents for seven days so that you can get the experience of running an auction. However, for the most part, I would suggest you list your items at *Fixed Price*. As I said earlier, that gives people plenty of time to find your listing and hopefully buy your item.

Next up is **Duration**. If you are running an auction, you can choose one, three, five, seven, or ten days. I prefer seven days, as it gives buyers a whole week to find your listing. However, if I have a particularly desirable item, I might consider running it for as few as three days, knowing it will sell quickly.

In the **Price** field, you will either enter in your starting bid price or your fixed price. If you decide to run an auction, you will notice that you can offer a *Buy It Now* price. This means that while you have a starting auction price, you also set a *Buy It Now Fixed Price* that buyers who do not want to bid can take advantage of. So, if you start an auction at 99-cents, you could also offer a *Buy It Now* price of $9.99.

Note that extra fees apply if you offer a *Buy It Now* price on an auction listing. Also, if someone places a bid, the *Buy It Now* option will disappear, and all buyers will now have to bid on the item; no one can buy it outright. Because of the fees, you should only offer the *Buy It Now* option on auctions that you start at a higher price.

If you choose to list an item at *Fixed Price*, the only duration option now available is **Good 'Til Cancelled**, which means your item will automatically be relisted every 30 days until it sells or is manually ended. You will set your own *Buy It Now* price, and you can enable the *Best Offer* option.

Note that there is an option to schedule your listing to go live at a specific start time. While some experienced sellers choose to pay for scheduling their listings, most, including me, simply check the **Start my listing when I submit them** box.

You can also set a **Reserve** price that the winning buyer will have to meet for an additional fee. I prefer to start my auctions at the lowest price I will be happy with rather than pay additional fees to set up a *Reserve* price.

The **Best Offer** feature can be added to both *Auction* and *Fixed Price* listings. You can also set up automatic accept and decline amounts. However, it can be advantageous to let all offers, even insultingly low ones, come through as it keeps your store listings active in Ebay's algorithm. Ebay likes to see that customers engage with your listings, which helps your items get bumped up in search.

Quantity is simply the number of items you have for sale. If you are only selling one book, for instance, you just type in a "1". If you are selling multiple, identical copies of the same item – for instance, you have three copies of a video game – then you would type in the number of items you have. Note that multiple items must all be IDENTICAL, not only in that they are all exactly the same item but that the conditions are all the same, too. If you have two of the same shirts, one brand new with the tags and one that has been washed and worn, you will need to create two separate listings.

A **Private listing** allows your buyer's Ebay user names to be hidden, and the **Make a donation** option lets you donate a portion of your sales to the charity of your choice.

Under the **Payment options**, you can opt to **Require Immediate Payment When Buyer Uses Buy It Now**. This will prevent people from clicking on the item but then not paying for it. All of my *Fixed Price* listings require *Immediate Payment*. *Auctions* cannot have Immediate Payment unless you set up a Buy It Now price; if you accept or send offers, *Immediate Payment* will not be enabled, either.

In late 2019, Ebay began collecting **Sales tax** for the states that required it. I used to collect sales tax on all orders within my state and submit a quarterly payment; however, Ebay now takes care of this for all sellers. Since the sales tax field is still in the listing templates, I still check the box even though I no longer must collect the tax myself.

Finally, you can set up your **Return options**. I currently do not accept returns, so I leave both the boxes for *Domestic returns* and *International returns* unchecked. However, if you decide to accept returns, you can choose whether the buyer has 14, 30, or 60 days to contact you; and you can decide whether you or the buyer will pay the return postage.

In recent years, Ebay has heavily pressured sellers to offer "free returns," meaning sellers PAY the return postage. However, most sellers, including me, cannot afford to absorb the cost of returns. Whether or not you choose to accept returns and whether you choose to make them "free" is only a decision you can make.

Next is the **Shipping** section; we will cover this in-depth in the next chapter. But, as an overview, you will first decide which of the **Domestic shipping options** you want to select for your listing:

- **Flat:** Same cost to all buyers
- **Calculated:** Cost varies by buyer location
- **Freight:** Large items over 150 lbs.
- **No shipping:** Local pickup only

Likely, you will be deciding between either *Flat* or *Calculated* shipping. In the example using the shirt, let's say you have weighed the top on your digital scale and know that it is light enough to ship via *USPS First Class Mail*, which is under $6. So, for the shirt, you choose the *Flat: Same cost to all buyer's option* and select *USPS First Class* under *Services* with the cost of $5.99. Again, I will cover all the shipping methods further in the next chapter of this book; but we will stick with this example for now.

The next section you will need to select is your **Handling time.** Ebay offers you the option to ship the very same day all the way up to thirty days. I select two business days from the drop-down menu of options. While I almost always ship out the following business day, giving customers a two-day time frame allows me a bit of wiggle room to get the package out.

Under the **Package weight & dimensions** section, you will choose **Package (or thick envelope)** from the options presented; and you will want to enter some general numbers into the **Dimensions** section. You do not have to be exact here; you just want to let Ebay know that you will be shipping the item in a regular-sized package, not something oversized. I usually just enter 10x10x10 into this space as that size falls under the maximum size of 16x16x16.

Under **Weight,** you can enter the package's exact weight, although I advise selecting one of the pounds ranges Ebay offers you. You already know that it is under one pound for the shirt, so you would select *1 lb. or less* from the drop-down menu.

The last section of the listing template is **Sell it faster**, which is where you can choose **Promoted Listings** and **Volume Pricing**. We will discuss these further along in this book.

At the bottom of the page, Ebay will show you the **Fees** associated with your listing. And finally, unless you want to *Preview your listing* or *Save as a draft*, you can click on the **large blue List item button** to make your listing go live on Ebay's site. And then you just sit back and wait for it to sell!

Your Second Listing: Once you have gotten one Ebay listing under your belt, the second one will be super easy to complete as the first listing created a template for all your future listings. Now when you are ready to create a new listing, you simply open a listing that is either active or has ended, then click on **Sell Similar.**

What *Sell Similar* does is copy the information from the original listing into a new listing. Then you only need to change the title, photos, item specifics, and shipping weight for your new item. If you list the item in the same category as the first, you will not even have to change that section, which is why listing goes much faster if you list like items back-to-back as you will have fewer specifics to alter. Plus, you do not have to recreate every one of your settings with every single new listing.

However, let's say the first Ebay listing you created was for a book. You have created that listing, and it is live on Ebay's website. Now you want to list a coat. You simply click on the listing for the book and then click on *Sell Similar* at the top left-hand corner of the listing. A new page will open that will look exactly like the book listing, but you can now edit it. Change the fields that will make the coat's listing instead of the book: *Title, Category, Condition, Photos* (make sure you delete the old photos before uploading the new ones), *Item Specifics, Item Description, Selling Details, and Shipping Details.* Once you have adjusted the fields to reflect the coat's information, you can then just click on the List item icon to make the listing go live. And if you have another item to list, you can simply click on *Sell Similar* in the coat listing!

Back to the book example: Perhaps you had the book listed at *Auction* with the buyer paying for calculated *Media Mail* shipping. However, for the coat, you want to list it at *Fixed Price* with "Free Shipping." Note that you will need to change the selling format and the shipping options within the new listing. However, you do not have to worry about changing your return policy or excluded shipping locations as those carried over from the book listing.

Under *Shipping Details*, since you are doing *Calculated Shipping* and have set up those specifics in your first listing, you only need to change the item's weight and how you will ship it. Since clothing cannot go *Media Mail,* and because the coat weighs over a pound, you will have to choose *Parcel* or *Priority*. I give my customers a choice: the lower cost *Parcel* and the more expensive *Priority*. The customer feels they are getting a deal with the "free" *Parcel* shipping option I am offering in this instance, but they can also pay to upgrade to *Priority* if they want the coat faster.

As you did with the first listing, you simply hit the **List item** icon after you have changed all the relative fields and added in the new photos. You can then open that listing, click on *Sell Similar* again, and start on your next listing.

The *Sell Similar* trick is fast and easy; I cannot remember the last time I created a new listing from scratch. Note that you can access the *Sell Similar* feature in a listing by either clicking on it or viewing all your listings on your *My Ebay* page. When looking at your *My Ebay* page, you will see a drop-down menu next to all your listings. One of the choices there is *Sell Similar*.

The listing process gets easier and faster with every new item you list. While it can be overwhelming at first, trust me that you will be listing items like a pro in no time. And when you are ready to take things to the next level, here are some of my advanced listing tips:

Research: Before I list anything on Ebay, I first research it to see what the going price for the item currently is; or if it is even selling at all. The way I do this is by doing a completed listing search. I simply type in a general description of my item in the search bar (for instance, "Pink Pyrex Bowl"), and I then narrow down the search fields, which appear on the screen's left side. Included in those search fields is one for **Completed Listings.** Selecting *Completed Listings* will show me what, if anything, an item has recently sold for.

If a completed listing search brings up several hundred listings, I will further narrow it down by selecting the **Sold** listings. Instead of showing me every item listed in the past few months, regardless of whether it sold or not, selecting *Sold* will only show me the listings that resulted in a sale. I can then sort the results using several options, including most recently ended, distance, or price; I prefer to sort using the highest price so that I can see which items sold for the most money. Note the price will also include shipping, regardless of whether the buyer or seller paid for it.

Since you are reading this book to grow your Ebay business, I assume that you have or plan to get an Ebay Store subscription. I will discuss the benefits of opening an Ebay Store later in this book, but I want to cover now one of the main bonuses of having a store: **Terapeak.**

Ebay acquired *Terapeak*, which is an online database of Ebay sales data, in 2017. *Terapeak* is now available for FREE to all Ebay Store subscribers.

Terapeak takes researching sold Ebay listings up a notch by providing you with an entire year's worth of data. While the

Completed Listing search on Ebay only gives you three months of sales records, with *Terapeak,* you can see what an item has been selling for during the previous twelve months. This is incredibly useful when you are researching off-season items. For instance, when you are listing Christmas items in May, *Terapeak* will show you what those items were selling for leading up to the previous holiday. I always advocate listing items whenever you have the time, not waiting until a specific season comes around. And if you are willing to sit on an item for a while, *Terapeak* allows you to set the highest selling price and wait for the right buyer to come along.

You can easily access *Terapeak* under the **Research** tab at the top of your **Seller Hub**. Trust me when I tell you that once you start utilizing *Terapeak* to research completed listings, you will never go back to the traditional Ebay search method!

When you are researching sold listings, whether via *Terapeak* or through Ebay's completed listings search, you will often find that your item has sold for a wide range of prices. This is when you need to examine the results to see why some sold for a high price while others only sold for a few dollars, if at all. Sometimes, the seller had a low asking price, either starting an item at auction for only 99-cents or listing it at *Fixed Price* for just a few dollars. Perhaps the pictures in the listing were terrible, or maybe the item itself was in awful condition. Compare the highest sold price listing with the lowest one to determine what factored into the difference. And then price your item accordingly.

If my item is in the same condition as the listing that sold for the highest price, I base my price on that listing. I also note *when* the item was sold to account for seasonality. Back to the example of Christmas items: If I am listing a Christmas collectible, I want to base my price on what it sold for during the previous holiday season, not what it may have sold for during the summer months. I am willing to let them sit in my store for some items, specifically vintage collectibles, until the right buyer comes along. The exception to this is clothing, as I prefer to move clothes much faster, specifically if it is a trendy piece that may go out of style if it is listed too long.

Note that it is imperative to base the selling price of the item you are listing on the comparable sales results and conditions. While a brand-new book may bring in top dollar, a used one may only bring in a few bucks. Ensure that you base your item's price on those in a similar condition to yours when looking at the completed listing results. Remember that "brand new" refers to items with absolutely no flaws. The original tags attached, basically, in the condition it was in as it rolled off the manufacturing line. However, most of the items you will sell on Ebay are likely to be secondhand, and condition plays a huge factor in how much pre-owned items will sell for.

I also use the *Terapeak* and Ebay search results to tell me if an item usually only sells with "free" shipping. As I say in every Ebay book that I have ever written, shipping is never actually "free" as someone, either the seller or the buyer, must pay for the postage.

However, some categories, such as clothing, are so crowded and competitive that building the cost of postage into the asking price to list the item with "free" shipping is often necessary to get the sale. Health and beauty items are also products that typically sell best when listed with "free" shipping. And if you sell similar items, offering "free" shipping may help convince a buyer to purchase multiple items from you as they will not be wondering about the shipping charges.

While I typically research pricing on my computer, I sometimes look up items on my smartphone using Ebay's mobile app when I am out and about. That way, I can quickly find if an item is worth picking up or if I should pass on it. The downside to using Ebay Mobile for me is that I often run into problems finding an internet connection (especially when I am at an estate sale in the country). I have even had difficulty getting an internet connection inside Goodwill stores.

So, while it would be nice to look up every item before I buy it, I often must rely on instinct and wait until I return to my office to do any research. If the item you are researching has a bar code, you can use the Ebay app to scan it in to check on its current price. Note that if the Ebay app is not working for you for whatever reason, you can also use the Amazon Seller app for scanning purposes.

Remember that an item is only worth what someone will pay for it. Therefore, looking at the *active* Ebay listings will not be much help as those results only show what sellers are currently ASKING for the item. The *completed listings* will show you what customers have actually paid for the item. This is often the biggest mistake new Ebay sellers make; they only look at the active listings, not the sold results. I also hear this a lot from people selling their items at garage sales. "It's selling for $1000 on Ebay!" they will claim, but they have usually only looked at the active listings, not the sold results.

Some categories, specifically clothing, require you to list the size of the item you are selling. While most clothing sizes are straightforward, I sometimes need to research how various clothing brands size their garments. For instance, Chicos, a women's clothing company, has its own unique sizing chart ranging from 000 (extra small) to 4.5 (extra-large). I also often have to research whether a piece of clothing is vintage (say, a pair of Levi's jeans) and how to spot counterfeit items (such as telling an authentic Coach purse from a fake).

I also pick up vintage items from overseas that are not labeled in English; fortunately, Google can quickly translate most languages to English. I have found several German Bibles and hymnals over the years that I needed help translating, and I have also gotten pottery marked in a foreign language. I simply type in the book title or makers mark into the Google search bar, followed by "translate to English" to get a translation.

If you are dealing with vintage and collectible items like me, you may need to do further research on a piece to provide as much information about it as possible. For instance, I sell a lot of vintage flatware sets. These sell best when I can identify the pattern; so, I visit sites such as *replacements.com* to find the name, manufacturer, and date of the sets I am selling.

Again, a simple Google search will bring up all kinds of resources for most objects you are selling. Nearly every collectible item has at least one dedicated website, often run by actual collectors, that you can use to research everything from pottery to clothing.

Do not just rely on Ebay to do your research; use the World Wide Web to learn as much as possible about the items you are selling. Yes, all this research takes time; but remember that the more information you can provide in your listings, the more likely your item will sell fast and for top dollar!

Auction vs. Fixed Price: What makes Ebay such a unique selling platform is the different ways you can sell items. You can run **Auctions** from one to ten days, and you can also, for an added fee, include a **Buy It Now** price to your auction listing. Or you can list items at **Fixed Price.** While Ebay used to allow you to list items for a set period, now all *Fixed Price* items are listed **Good 'Til Cancelled.**

Then there is the **Best Offer** option, which you can add to both *Auction* and *Fixed Price* listings. *Best Offer* allows potential buyers to send you a direct offer on your item. You can either accept, decline, or negotiate with a Counteroffer. You can also set up **Automatic Accept** and **Automatic Decline** options to instantly agree to or decline offers that meet or do not meet the thresholds you have set.

There are so many choices, I know! But the bottom line is that all Ebay listings, despite the length and added options, will either be *Auctions* or *Fixed Price*. Many Ebay sellers start out selling their items using one format and get stuck using the same option for all their listings. However, some items sell better at *Auction,* while others do best at *Fixed Price*. But how do you know whether you should start an item at *Auction* or just list it at *Fixed Price*? The answer depends on the item itself.

If you have done your research, using either Ebay's *Completed Listing* search or *Terapeak*, and found that the item you are selling commands a steady price of, say, $50 on Ebay, then go ahead and list yours for $50 at *Fixed Price*. If you find your item sells for a wide range of prices, you may want to price yours in the middle.

As I discussed earlier in this book, condition is a huge factor in pricing your items. If the items you see selling for top-dollar are in like-new condition, but the item you are listing is in poor condition, you need to price accordingly.

However, if you see that the item typically brings in many bidders at *Auction*, you may want to try listing yours at *Auction*, too. While you can run an Ebay *Auction* from one to ten days, I prefer listing them for seven days. Seven days gives potential customers an entire week to find your item listing and decide if they want to bid.

As far as adding the *Buy It Now* option to auctions, I rarely do this as you must pay an additional fee; and I try to keep my Ebay fees as low as possible. If I have a good idea of how much an item will sell for, I just list it at *Fixed Price* rather than bother with an *Auction* as, again, I am only doing *Auctions* for items I have no idea how to price or because I want to get them out of my inventory.

Note that if you have a particularly "hot" item that you have started at *Auction*, you will likely receive messages asking you to sell the item outright. This is a tell-tale sign that you should keep the item at *Auction* just as you listed it as it indicates just how desirable it is. And it is also a good reminder that you were wise not to have added a *Buy It Now* option as the bidding will likely go higher than the price you would have set.

If I think an item should realistically sell for $19.99, I will not list it at *Auction* for $9.99 with a $19.99 *Buy It Now* price as the item would likely end up only selling for $9.99, anyway. And if an item has the potential of selling for $50, I will not start it at an *Auction* of $9.99 with a *Buy It Now* of $19.99 as I am severely limiting my profit potential. In both cases, adding in the *Buy It Now* option would not only result in my items likely selling for less money, but I would also have to pay additional listing fees for the extra feature.

While Ebay started as an auction site, the landscape has changed a lot over the years. It is now tough to get the price you want for an item when you start it as an *Auction* as customers are becoming used to and now typically prefer to buy things at a set price rather than bidding on something and then having to wait up to a week to see whether they win. More than ever before, Ebay is in direct competition with Amazon and Walmart, so you need to adjust your selling strategies to meet the changing times continually.

While I typically stick to listing my Ebay items at *Fixed Price*, I will occasionally use *Auctions* to clear out stale inventory, especially clothing. *Auctions* are an excellent way to bring in traffic to my Ebay Store, and even if someone does not bid on anything I have up at *Auction*, they may end up checking out my other listings and buying one of my *Fixed Price* items.

Best Offer: When you list an item at *Fixed Price* on Ebay, you have the option of allowing buyers to send you offers via the *Best Offer* feature. There is no additional fee associated with adding the *Best Offer* option to your listings. You can add *Best Offer* to all or only some of your listings, and you can also remove it at any time if you change your mind. It is easy to add *Best Offer* to your listings; you can do so individually within the listing itself by checking the box under the price to enable customers to submit offers to you.

If you want to add *Best Offer* to multiple listings, the **Bulk Edit** feature makes adding and removing options such as *Best Offer* easy; just go to your **Seller Hub** and click on **Listings**. Select **Active** from the drop-down menu and click on the boxes next to the listings you want to edit. Then click on **Edit** and select **Edit Selected** from the drop-down menu. You will then be taken to a page when you can bulk add, edit, or remove features, including price, payment, and shipping.

When dealing with *Best Offer,* note that you can choose to accept or decline offers automatically, or you can choose to review each offer personally. For instance, if you have an item priced at $50, you can choose to accept any offer of $40 or more automatically; and you can choose to decline any offers under $24.99 automatically. However, as I said, you can leave the settings open to review every offer. Some sellers prefer to review all offers manually and never set up an auto-decline price as they believe that it is best to attempt to negotiate with anyone who sends an offer. However, what you decide to do is up to you.

When you get an offer on an item, you have 48 hours to review it and respond. You can accept the offer, and the buyer will automatically be committed to completing the purchase. Many Ebay sellers such as myself hope that once all users are enrolled in Ebay's *Managed Payments* system, buyers who submit a Best Offer will have their funds automatically sent to the seller rather than initiate payment. Poshmark allows buyers to submit offers to sellers. If the seller accepts the offer, Poshmark immediately charges the customer for the purchase and sends the seller a label to ship out the item. On Ebay, however, buyers still must submit payment manually. And while most customers do pay, there are, of course, those who do not. Hopefully, this is something that Ebay will eventually be able to enact via *Managed Payments*.

Back to receiving a *Best Offer:* Note that you can also outright refuse any offers, closing the communication between you and the buyer. If that buyer wants to send you another offer, they will have to start the *Best Offer* process again. Some buyers like to send ridiculously low offers, such as offering $1 for a $50 item. These people obviously have no genuine interest in buying the item, so I do not engage with them; I simply decline their offer. If they continue to message me or submit more low offers, I will block them.

However, if you get a reasonable offer, you can choose to send the customer a counteroffer; most sellers send counteroffers for reasonable offers from buyers who they suspect really want the item. Let's go back to that $50 item. You have it listed at *Fixed Price* with the *Best Offer* option. A potential customer sends you an offer of $30. You can then send a counteroffer of, say, $40. If the buyer accepts, they are then required by Ebay to complete the transaction for the item. However, the customer may want to continue negotiating by submitting a counteroffer to you of $35; again, you can accept this or counteroffer yourself, either for your original $40 offer or for one a couple of dollars less, say $38.

Sometimes, however, counteroffers are not accepted or completely ignored. While this can be frustrating, it is just a part of the unique Ebay selling platform. Don't get discouraged by customers who send low-ball offers or refuse your counteroffers; move on, and eventually, the right buyer will come along. Just the fact that someone has engaged with your listing by sending an offer helps the item show up higher in Ebay's search algorithm as the action tells the Ebay system that people are interested in the item and that it has the potential to sell. And at the end of the day, Ebay is a business; they want your items to sell just as much as you do so that they can charge you *Final Value Fees* on top of your *Insertion Fees* and *Store Subscription Fees.*

Note that you want to carefully review all offers to ensure the offer does not include a change to the shipping price. I have had buyers send me an offer that also stipulated I would give them free shipping. For instance, they would offer me $5 plus free shipping for an item I had listed for $10, with the buyer paying the postage cost. Had I accepted those terms, I would have essentially had to PAY to ship them the item. So, be very careful to understand the terms you agree to when you accept a *Best Offer.*

As far as adding the *Best Offer* option to my listings, I only do this after an item has been listed for a month or so. If I list something for $50 and after 30 days it hasn't sold, I might end the listing and then relist it (using the **Sell Similar** option to show up as a brand-new listing on Ebay's site) in the *Best Offer* option. I typically do not do this the first time around as I want to try for the maximum selling price, and when you have the *Best Offer* option active, most customers are likely to try and negotiate.

I set my *Best Offer* listings to automatically decline any offer that is less than 50% of my asking price. If I were willing to take half for an item, I would just list it for that. As for which offers I will accept, I look carefully at the item itself, what I originally paid for it, how long I have had it listed, and what I think it should go for. I will generally accept offers of 25% or less off my asking price; if the offer is between 26-51% off my asking price, I will usually send a counteroffer to try to get closer to the 25% off mark. However, some sellers happily engage with any customer who sends offers. What you decide to do is up to you and how much time (and patience!) you have for fielding offers.

I only negotiate sale prices using the official Ebay *Best Offer* feature; I do NOT accept offers or make deals using the Ebay messaging system or with people who email me directly. It is very common for buyers to message sellers directly with their offer terms, including requests for free shipping; I generally just ignore these messages or reply telling them that I only negotiate on items that have the *Best Offer* option on them.

Do not let potential customers bully you into selling your items for less. Buyers who send direct messages asking for a discount usually do so because they know that the item is indeed worth what you have listed it for, and they are trying to snatch it away before another buyer comes along. Or if you have the item up for *Auction*, they know that it will have multiple bidders and are trying to get you to sell it to them outright, so they do not have to compete in a bidding war.

Offers To Watchers: A recent feature to Ebay's site is sellers' ability to send offers to interested customers. When someone "watches" an Ebay item, Ebay allows the seller to send an offer. You can choose a percentage or a set amount of the item's price, and the customer has 48 hours to accept. You can also enable the customer to submit a counteroffer. Sellers do not see the user's name of the person they send the offer to.

For me, *Offers To Watchers* has proven to be the most effective way to generate a sale. It has worked better for me than either allowing buyers to submit offers or running sales in my store. I typically send offers out once or twice a week. Ebay makes sending offers incredibly easy. When you access your *Active Listings* in your *Seller Hub*, you will see a highlighted **Send offers – eligible** button highlighted above your listings. Clicking on this will take you to a new page to see all the items that currently have watchers.

You can choose to send offers through each individual listing, or you can send offers on all the items by bulk selecting all the listings, clicking on the **Send Offer** button, and choosing your terms. You can choose to offer a percentage off or a dollar amount off. Although Ebay provides an automated "Here's your chance to get this item at a great price!" option, you can add a personalized message. And you can also allow counteroffers from those to who you send offers.

Buyers have 48 hours to either decline or accept offers, although they can, and often do, just ignore them. And while many customers do not respond to offers, they may not be interested in purchasing your item but are instead either watching it as they plan to sell a similar item or are just curious to seee what it eventually sells for. So, don't be discouraged if you send out several offers and get no response. I still get enough of a response from customers who are actually interested in purchasing the items that it is worth it to me to send out offers regularly.

Pricing: While I do a completed listing search for every item I list on Ebay to determine a price, I tend to stick to a few key price points: $9.99, $24.99, $49.99, and $99.99. I choose these amounts for two reasons: One, these were the price points Ebay used to charge different fees for back when I first started selling on their site, and while they no longer do this, it was this way for years, and I've yet to break the habit. Two, customers have been trained over time to look for prices ending in 99-cents. After all, aren't you more willing to buy something priced at $24.99 instead of $26.45? When a customer chooses between spending UNDER $25 or OVER $25, even if the difference is only pennies and the shipping is more expensive or slower, they are more likely to spend the price point under the threshold.

Sticking to these price points has worked well for me over the years. Of course, if I have done my research and found that an item is selling for a different amount, I will undoubtedly price it accordingly. And I will also accept offers or run sales for lesser amounts. These numbers are my base prices, not always my final prices.

Many sellers will price items at $9.97 or $24.98, hoping that their items will appear before $9.99 or $24.99 in Ebay searches. However, it is essential to remember that Ebay shows items based on the *total* price, including shipping. So, if your shipping is higher than the competition, your listing will still appear after other listings despite any difference in the price of the item itself.

For auctions, I generally will not start the bidding lower than $9.99 unless I know for sure that I have a very desirable item OR if I just want to move stale inventory. If you start your auction at 99-cents, do so only if you are using the auction to draw traffic to your other listings, you are trying to move old items, or if you are confident that a bidding war will ensue. Otherwise, don't be upset when your item only sells for 99-cents.

Ebay is flooded with 99-cent items, so be careful not to devalue your items by getting them lumped into the 99-cent listings that permeate the site. Even upping your starting bid to $1.99 or $2.99 will help cover your fees if your item only sells for the opening bid. And you can always add a dollar or two to your shipping fee to act as a buffer. I have seen many successful sellers run 99-cent auctions with a $9.99 shipping charge to ensure that all fees are covered and that they make a small profit.

The bottom line is that you want to price your items at the amount you will be happy with. If you want at least $20 for something, do not start the auction at $5; start it at $19.99. I see so many new sellers lose money by pricing their items too low, both at *Auction* and *Fixed Price.* These sellers do not make as much money, and the item itself gets devalued across the board. Again, do your research to determine what your item goes for on average and price yours accordingly. You may realize that it is almost always best for you to list them at *Fixed Price* for the types of items you sell so you make precisely what the item is worth.

Immediate Payment: One way to protect yourself from customers clicking to buy your items but not paying is to require *Immediate Payment*. This can only be done on *Fixed Price* items, not *Auctions*, and not on *Best Offer*, either from a buyer sending you an offer or with you using *Offers To Watchers*. And it may not be practical for you if you are a seller that frequently sells multiple items in the same transaction as it prevents you from combining a customer's order. For instance, if you specialize in golf accessories, you may sell several items in one transaction to the same customer; and sending them an invoice with combined shipping is essential.

However, if you are like me and sell primarily unique, individual items, requiring *Immediate Payment* can save you the hassle of dealing with non-paying buyers. The option to require *Immediate Payment* is available under the *Payment* section of all Ebay listings. I tend to be somewhat flexible on putting *Immediate Payment* on my listings by only using it for high-priced items. For small items under $10, I generally do not have *Immediate Payment* turned on as these are the items that are more likely to be purchased in multiples by the same customer. While one person may buy three $10 coffee mugs from me, it is rare that a single customer will come along and purchase three $100 silverware sets from my store simultaneously.

Discounts: You can set up automatic shipping discounts for customers who buy multiple items, either giving them a percentage or dollar-off discount or automatically providing free shipping when they spend a certain amount of money. This works best if all your items tend to be the same size and weight, for instance, if you sell CDs or miniatures. It is much easier to estimate shipping costs when all your products weigh roughly the same amount.

For example, you may set your shipping discounts to give customers free shipping when buying three or more items. Or you may give them $1 off for every item they buy after the first one. So, if they buy three $5 items, they will pay $5 for the first and then $4 each for the other two.

If you have an **Ebay Store**, you can set up these automatic discounts using the **Promotions Manager** under the **Marketing Tab** in **Seller Hub**. For items to be eligible for *Promotions*, the listing must be in a *Fixed Price* format with *Buy It Now* pricing. Items will appear at the advertised price, and the discount will be applied to the buyer's shopping cart. You can offer five different types of offers using *Promotions Manager*:

- **Order discounts:** Offer discounts based on order size or the amount spent by a buyer. You can also create promotions such as a percentage off an additional item or a buy-one-get-one-free offer.
- **Codeless coupons:** Offer exclusive discounts to buyer groups of your choosing by using a virtual coupon.
- **Promotional shipping:** Offer cheaper shipping on items that qualify for your offer.
- **Sales events:** Reduce prices for selected items or categories.
- **Volume price discounts:** Offer tiered discounts to buyers who purchase multiple quantities of a single item.

CHAPTER EIGHT:

EBAY SHIPPING MADE EASY

Now for the most confusing part of selling on Ebay for new sellers: Shipping! While I touched on shipping in several previous parts of this book, in this chapter, I will dig into the topic and walk you step-by-step through all your options, including how to print your shipping labels. This chapter has some overlap from earlier in this book, but readers have asked for a dedicated section where everything is located, so here it is!

There are dozens of carriers and ways you can ship packages. While UPS and FedEx are viable shipping options, you will want to stick with shipping your packages through the United States Postal Service (USPS) when you are just starting out. The USPS provides the best value and service for small sellers, and Ebay has partnered with them to make shipping easy and cost-effective. Since the USPS is Ebay's preferred shipping partner, if you sell on Ebay, you will be using them a lot.

While there are numerous ways you can ship a package through the Post Office, most Ebay sellers ship via one of four methods, all of which are for shipments within the United States (including San Juan, Puerto Rico, and military bases):

- **Media Mail**
- **First Class Mail**
- **Parcel Select**
- **Priority Mail**

Media Mail: Media Mail is for, surprise, MEDIA! It is preferable to ship books via *Media Mail* because they are heavy, and you get a discounted rate. However, the low price also means that *Media Mail* is extremely slow, sometimes taking up to one month (although the Post Office claims delivery is two to eight business days).

The following items qualify to be shipped via *Media Mail*:

- Books of at least eight printed pages
- 16-millimeter or narrower width films and catalogs of films 24 pages or more
- Printed music
- Educational testing materials and printed educational materials
- Sound recordings
- Playscripts and manuscripts
- Loose-leaf pages and their binders of education medical information
- Computer-readable media

Media Mail can NOT be used for advertising, video games, computer drives, or digital drives. The maximum weight for a *Media Mail* package is 70-pounds.

Some sellers try to cheat the system by shipping heavy, non-media items via *Media Mail.* This is a violation of the USPS policy and can result in you losing your postal account. Post offices are notorious for opening boxes marked as *Media Mail* to ensure they only contain approved media items, so be careful to follow the rules.

***Media Mail* items can only be shipped in plain boxes or envelopes**, NOT in the *Priority Mail* boxes. When you print a label via Ebay (more on how to do this coming up), it will clearly state on the label which service you paid for. So, if you print a *Media Mail* label, it will say "MEDIA MAIL" at the top.

First Class: *First Class MAIL* is the service you use when you send a postcard or letter weighing 3.5-ounces or less. While one stamp equals one ounce on a rectangular postcard or letter up to 3.5-ounces, anything 4-ounces or larger is charged at a higher PACKAGE RATE. Unless you are selling postcards or brochures that fit in standard letter envelopes, you will be paying the package rate to ship your Ebay orders.

You can ship up to 16-ounces (1-pound) via *First Class*. Like *Media Mail*, **First Class packages must be in plain boxes or envelopes;** you can NOT use the free *Priority Mail* boxes or envelopes to ship *First Class* packages.

Shipping items via *First Class* is where having a digital postal scale really comes in handy as you can get your package down to the exact ounce. The *First Class* cost varies by weight and zone, so it is essential to get as close a weight on your item as possible (I will talk more about weighing your packages coming up). If you are using *Calculated Shipping* and having your customers pay the shipping charge, offering them *First Class* postage saves them money. If the package you are sending weighs 8-ounces, the difference between *First Class* and *Parcel* or *Priority* can be as much as $6, depending on where the item is shipping to.

You save a significant amount on postage when you print your labels directly through Ebay. Not only do you get a discount for shipping online, but your seller level can also mean you get an extra discount. Knowing exactly how much a package weighs will help you keep control of your postage costs.

However, even with a digital scale, finding the exact ounce can be challenging as you need an item's weight before you list an item. My trick when dealing with items that will ship in poly mailers, and one that I will talk more about later in this book, is to add 3-ounces to the weight of these light packages to account for packing materials. So, if you have a small item that, on its own, weighs 5-ounces, list it as 8-ounces. That way, when it is in an envelope with bubble wrap and a packing slip, you will not risk the Post Office sending it back for insufficient postage.

Since I typically offer "free shipping" on my items, I do not have to worry about what I am charging the customer. I weigh my items before I list them so that I know how much to pad the item price to account for shipping, and I weigh them again when I ship them to get the actual postage cost. Yes, I add in the postage cost to my "free" listings as shipping is NOT "free"; someone, in this case, me, must pay for it. Buyers, however, like "free shipping," so this little trick works to not only entice customers but to avoid complaints about postage costs.

Parcel Select: *Parcel Select*, formerly called *Parcel Post*, is for packages weighing over 16-ounces. *Parcel* is slower than *Priority* (shipping time can take up to two weeks, although the Post Office claims two to eight business days), but it is cheaper for heavy shipments. **Parcel shipments must be in plain boxes or envelopes**; just as with *Media Mail* and *First Class*, you can NOT ship *Parcel Select* shipments in the *Priority Mail* boxes. The maximum weight for *Parcel* packages is 70-pounds.

Parcel Select postage cost depends on the weight of the package and where it is going. That is why it is wise to use Ebay's *Calculated Shipping* as the customer pays for the exact shipping for their zip code.

While *Parcel Select* is an excellent option for heavy packages, you want to make sure to check the cost between *Parcel* and *Priority* when you are creating your shipping label through Ebay (again, I will be going over how to do this coming up). Depending on how far away the package is going, *Priority Mail* may be the cheaper option.

For example, I am in Iowa, centrally located on both coasts in the middle of the country. For packages weighing less than four pounds, it is often cheaper for me to ship via *Priority Mail* over *Parcel Select*. Plus, I get to use a free *Priority Mail* shipping box, and I get a discount on postage by shipping directly through Ebay.

What is great about shipping through Ebay is you can look at all the package and price options before paying for and printing a label. That way, I can find the best rate AND fastest shipping time for each order. It is always nice when a customer pays for *Parcel,* but you can upgrade them to *Priority*. Not only do you save money, but the item arrives much faster. Don't worry; I will be going over how to do this later in this book.

Priority Mail: *Priority Mail* is for packages weighing over 16-ounces or more that need to get to their location quickly, typically 2-3 business days. Note that "business days" means weekdays and does not include Saturdays, Sundays, or federal holidays. If you ship an item out on a Friday, realize that it may not be processed and scanned at your area Post Office until Monday. From there, it will have an additional two to three days before it reaches the customer.

As I explained above, when talking about *Parcel Select*, sometimes *Priority Mail* can be the cheaper option. For me, this is often true for packages weighing less than four pounds that are going as far as the East coast. I also get a shipping discount because I ship directly through Ebay, and I get the *Priority Mail* boxes for free. In fact, most of my shipments go via *Priority Mail* as nine times out of ten, it ends up being the cheapest option for packages between one and four pounds.

Priority Mail has other bonuses over *Parcel Select,* including FREE tracking when you purchase the label online, Saturday delivery, and FREE **Carrier Pickup.** I utilize *Carrier Pickup* to have my mail carrier pick up my packages and scan them in immediately; however, I must have at least one *Priority Mail* or *First Class* package to request a pickup. If I have all *Parcel Select* packages, for example, I cannot request this free pickup service. Since I work from home, *Carrier Pickup* is a blessing as I do not have to make multiple trips to the Post Office every week!

Of course, the best thing about *Priority Mail* is the FREE boxes! There are many sizes of *Priority Mail* boxes, including *Regular, Flat Rate,* and *Regional Rate* options. They also have *Flat Rate Bubble Mailers,* which are extremely handy. Suppose you are just starting out on Ebay. In that case, I recommend ordering 10-count packages of all the available boxes and envelopes (JUST the regular *Priority* and *Flat Rate* options, not the *Express* and *Overnight* versions) so that you will have an adequate supply on hand. Not only are the boxes FREE, but your postal carrier will deliver them right to your door for FREE, too!

While the Post Office promotes their *Flat Rate* boxes and envelopes as having the best postage costs, regular *Priority Mail* is usually cheaper for packages less than four pounds. Why? When it comes to Priority Mail, it is not just the weight but also the distance a package has to travel.

As I mentioned previously, I live in Iowa. I can send a two-pound package to Minnesota for a little over $7. However, that same package costs over $10 to ship to California. If that package is going to New York, the postage is around $9. To Hawaii or Alaska, the cost jumps to $13. Again, it is not just the weight, but the distance the package must travel.

The type of *Priority Mail* box (*Regular, Flat Rate,* or *Regional*) does not affect the speed of delivery. *Priority* is *Priority.* The difference in the shipping cost depends on the type and size of the box.

Regular Priority Mail: A regular *Priority Mail* box is priced by weight and the zip code to which it is being shipped. You can ship *Priority Mail* packages in regular boxes and envelopes, too, not only in the branded *Priority* boxes. The label that prints off from Ebay is branded as *Priority.* Still, we also keep *Priority Mail* stickers (again, FREE from the Post Office) on hand to ensure the package is easily spotted as *Priority* as the postal carriers do their initial package sorting. The stickers are also nice for covering up writing on boxes that we are repurposing.

The maximum weight for a *Priority Mail* package is 70-pounds. If you are using your own box, note that the maximum combined length and girth are 108-inches, which means the combined measurement of the longest side and the distance around the package's thickest part cannot be more than 108-inches. A more straightforward calculation is not to use a box that measures larger than 12x12x12-inches. I keep a small supply of 14x14x14-inch and 16x16x16-inch boxes on hand, but I ship via *UPS Ground* for those sizes. With increasing postage rates and limits on box sizes, these days, I try to stick to items that fit in 12x12x12-inch boxes or smaller, just to make my life easier!

As I mentioned, the Post Office provides FREE *Priority Mail* stickers to put on plain boxes and envelopes. I keep a roll of stickers on hand for when we ship *Priority* packages in plain boxes. But don't feel that you must use the stickers; the shipping labels are designated as *Priority.* The *Priority* stickers are just another shipping supply item we like to keep on hand.

Flat Rate Priority Mail: *Flat Rate* boxes have a set price. You can pack them up to 70-pounds and pay one flat rate no matter where the package is going. However, there are various sizes of *Flat Rate* boxes and envelopes, each with its own price. The Post Office is continuously raising prices, but as of this writing, the envelopes and small boxes start at around $7, the medium boxes ship for a bit over $14, and the large box ships for nearly $20. The price varies depending on whether you print the labels yourself on Ebay or at USPS.com (cheaper) or have the Post Office print them for you (more expensive).

While the Post Office heavily promotes *Flat Rate* boxes as the best option, *Flat Rate* is often more expensive than shipping via regular *Priority*. For instance, say you have a ceramic dish that weighs three pounds once it is in a shipping box. If you put it in a *Medium Flat Rate* box, it will cost over $14 to ship anywhere in the country. Now, if you are in Florida and your buyer is in California, that works out to be a great deal. However, if your buyer lives in your state or in a surrounding one, you could save as much as $7 in postage by choosing regular *Priority Mail.*

Again, by using Ebay's shipping tool, you will be able to see and compare all the options available so that you can find the best deal on postage for each order. However, note that if a customer pays for *Priority*, you need to ship the item *Priority. Priority* is an *Expedited Service* and is the fastest option compared to *Media, First Class,* or *Parcel.* So, if your buyer pays for *Priority* but you downgrade them to *Parcel,* they are rightfully going to be angry.

Regional Priority Mail: *Regional Rate* boxes are a new offering from the Post Office. There are four different sizes available: **A1, A2, B1,** and **B2.** They also used to have a *C* option, but they have done away with those. I have found that the *A1* and *A2* boxes are often cheaper than the regular *Priority Mail* boxes for my shipments. I only keep the two sizes of the *A* boxes in stock as they are the only ones I use; I have not stocked the *B* boxes in months as I never used them.

The downsides to *Regional Rate* are that the boxes themselves are relatively small in size and have lower weight limits (15-pounds for the A and 20-pounds for the B boxes). However, I keep a supply on hand in case I find that they are the best option. Again, since I ship via Ebay, I can look at all the shipping options before purchasing a label. As postage rates have increased, I have found myself reaching for the *Regional Rate A* boxes more and more, especially since I am currently selling smaller items.

More About Priority Mail: When packages are sorted for shipment at the Post Office, the most expensive postage options go first as they are guaranteed space on the trucks and planes. *Overnight* and *Express* are obviously the most expensive since the customer is paying for one-to-two-day delivery. *Media Mail* and *Bulk Mail* (bulk mail is usually "junk" mail that is sent out in mass) are the cheapest and, therefore, the last packages to be put out for delivery. It is all about available space; the more room on the truck or plane, the more packages they will ship out.

The Post Office promotes *Priority Mail* as being delivered in two to three business days. Again, that is BUSINESS days, i.e., WEEKDAYS. While some large postal facilities process mail on the weekends, the vast majority do not. Mail and packages are not processed on federal holidays, either. Ebay stands behind sellers in shipping times when it comes to mailing out orders on weekends and holidays; keep these rules in mind if you have a customer demanding that the order they placed on Friday arrive by Monday!

After *Priority*, *First Class Mail* is the next class to be shipped out, followed by *Parcel Select*, and finally *Media Mail.* It is always in your best interest as a seller to use the fastest option available, depending on the price. The faster the customer receives their order, the happier they will be!

International Shipping: International shipping used to be such a massive headache that most sellers avoided it altogether. While you certainly do not need to ship to Canada, South America, or overseas, doing so will significantly increase your business. Fortunately, Ebay now offers its **Global Shipping Program**, an optional program you can opt into. Truth be told, Ebay will most likely put you in it whether you opt-in or not. I specifically opted OUT of the program twice, only to be put back in it. However, now that I am enrolled, it has been smooth sailing, and I kick myself for waiting so long to opt-in.

When a seller offers international shipping and opts into the *Global Shipping Program,* their international packages are sent to a sorting facility here in the United States. So, when I get an international shipment notification through *Global Shipping,* the label that prints out and the postage paid is to a Kentucky facility. After the package arrives at the facility, Ebay takes full responsibility for it, including filling out customs forms and putting on the postage to send to the buyer's country. Once a package reaches the Ebay facility, it is entirely in Ebay's hands, meaning if it is lost or if it arrives damaged, Ebay, not the seller, is responsible.

Because international shipping is now so easy using Ebay's *Global Shipping* program, there is no reason not to opt into it. Opening your sales to international customers will significantly increase your sales, and now printing a label is as easy as printing one for the United States.

However, some sellers still do prefer to ship internationally on their own. While I certainly do not recommend that new Ebay sellers who are struggling with shipping within the United States to try tackling international shipping, too, here are some essential points for those of you who at least want to know a bit more about how to ship your Ebay orders internationally if you are not using Ebay's *Global Shipping Program:*

- International orders ship via *First Class* (under four-pounds) or *Priority* (four-pounds or more)
- There are other services available, specifically *Express* and *Overnight*; however, in all my years of selling on Ebay, I have only ever had one international buyer request one of these faster services.

- While shipping a package via *First Class* to Canada may only cost a few dollars, most international shipments cost much more. Therefore, if you offer international shipping, you will want to ensure that the buyer is paying the postage cost to have the item delivered to their country.
- When you set up your domestic shipping, the same package weight and dimensions carry over to the international options. You only have to offer customers either *First Class* or *Priority*. Ebay's shipping calculator will figure out the postage cost based on the buyer's location. Let's say you are listing a coffee mug in the 1-2-pound range; you will offer *Parcel* or *Priority* for US customers and *First Class* or *Priority* for international customers. Ebay's *Shipping Calculator* will then do the rest.
- When you pay and print your shipping labels through Ebay, the shipping label, and the customs form will print out together. You simply sign the customs form and attach both the label and the customs form to your package.
- If you do not print your labels but instead take your packages to the Post Office for postage, note that you will need to fill out the customs forms there. The form requirements change frequently, so you will need a postal clerk to give you the correct forms and explain how to fill them out. This is just another reason you should print your shipping labels out yourself at home!
- Due to customs regulations in other countries, some buyers will ask you to mark their orders as a "Gift" to avoid paying customs fees. Note that this is illegal to do and could result in being suspended from using USPS services; be sure to tell any buyer who asks you to do this that you cannot and will not. Always mark international orders as "Merchandise." If the buyer persists, you can put in a cancellation order through Ebay under

the terms that the customer is asking you to violate a shipping policy.

Regardless of whether you ship international orders on your own or through Ebay's *Global Shipping* program, be aware that international packages' tracking varies greatly and is quite unreliable. More than the hassle of dealing with customs forms is the frustration of not always tracking international shipments. And without tracking, it is very easy for a customer to claim they never received their order, which means you will have to issue them a full refund. If you are shipping items on your own, you will ultimately be responsible for any lost or damaged packages. When you use Ebay's *Global Shipping,* however, Ebay is accountable for any shipping issues.

While Canada, the United Kingdom, and Australia all offer easy-to-track, generally reliable shipments, there are some areas of the world you may want to consider avoiding. Before I shipped through Ebay's *Global Shipping Program*, I blocked several countries and regions, including all Central and South America, all of Africa, all the Middle East, and Italy. While the other European countries offer fairly reliable shipping, Italy is notorious for holding packages up in customs and losing them. Mexico and the other South American counties also offer poor tracking, and shipping to anywhere in Africa or the Middle East is very risky as many online scams originate from those countries. Most international customers who buy from American Ebay sellers are in Canada, England, and Australia; for many years, those were the only areas I would sell to.

Once a shipment arrives in the country of the buyer, it first must go through customs. As I have mentioned, some countries do this very quickly, while others (Italy) are notoriously slow. International shipping can take as little as a week to arrive in Canada or up to a month or more for countries overseas. When I shipped internationally on my own, I always dealt with messages from overseas buyers wanting to know where their packages were. But by using Ebay's *Global Shipping*, I never hear from international customers as Ebay handles any questions about their packages.

So, those are the basics of shipping internationally on your own. While it can offer cost savings to the customer as they do not pay both you AND Ebay for postage, the time and confusion for new sellers can be too much. Doesn't using Ebay's *Global Shipping Program* sound much better? It is so easy, and Ebay protects you from lost or damaged packages. I will never go back to shipping internationally on my own!

How To Set Up Shipping In Your Listings: So, now that you understand the basic four categories of USPS shipping options, it is time to choose the ones you want to offer for your listings. One of the biggest mistakes new Ebay sellers make is to guess at shipping costs, resulting in either overcharging customers or undercharging them and losing money on shipping. However, using **Calculated Shipping** will protect you and your customers from incorrect postage costs.

I am a firm believer in using *Calculated Shipping* on Ebay for packages weighing over one pound. If you have a digital scale, there is no reason not to use it. *Calculated Shipping* means the buyer pays the exact shipping cost for the item's weight and the zip code it is being shipped to.

While more seasoned Ebay sellers like to experiment with "free" shipping (i.e., building the shipping cost into the price of an item), I recommend you stick to *Calculated Shipping* when you are just starting out and have the buyer pay shipping. This will protect you from LOSING money by trying to guess shipping costs. It also ensures a fair shipping rate for the customer, which will mean you will not get angry customers who figure they were overcharged for shipping. You can experiment with free shipping once you are more comfortable selling and shipping.

So, you have a digital postage scale and are ready to create a listing using *Calculated Shipping*. It is so easy to do; here is how:

First, put your item into a box similar to the one it will ship out in. Note that the box does not have to be the exact one you will end up shipping the item in; you just want a box close to the size and weight of the one you will be using. Boxes can easily add up to one pound of weight to a shipment, so you definitely need to know what box you will be using.

For example, if you are selling a coffee mug, place it in a 7x7x6-inch Priority Mail box or a similar-sized box. Set the box on the digital scale and note the weight. Perhaps it comes out to one-pound and four-ounces.

So, in the Ebay listing under package weight, you put in one-pound and four-ounces, right? WRONG! When you are dealing with weights above a pound (remember, sixteen-ounces or less can go via *First Class*; and since the mug is not a book, it cannot go via *Media Mail*), you do NOT need to know the EXACT weight; you only need to know the RANGE between pounds. Understanding that you only need to know the RANGE will make your shipping process go much more smoothly.

If a mug in a box weighs one-pound and four-ounces, you simply select the 1-2-pound range under *Calculated Shipping*. You do NOT need the exact ounces. In fact, because the box will actually weigh MORE than one-pound four-ounces when it ships out (due to packing materials), that initial weight will not be accurate, anyway.

See how easy it is when you only need to know the weight RANGE? 1-2 pounds, 2-3 pounds, 3-4 pounds, etc. When an item is being shipped via *Parcel Select, Priority Mail*, or *Media Mail*, you only need to know the RANGE of weight. There is no need to worry about being exact down to the ounce!

I mentally add three-ounces to small packages to account for packing materials. Yes, packing paper, newspaper, bubble wrap, packing peanuts, enclosures, and tape will add additional weight to the shipment. So, for the mug in the box that weighs in at one-pound and four-ounces, I mentally note the weight as one-pound and seven-ounces. However, I still do not need to put in that exact weight. I only need to put in that it is 1-2 pounds.

Note that larger breakables often need more packing materials than the three-ounce buffer will provide. So while my three-ounce trick works for small items, if I'm shipping something in a 12x12x12-inch box that will need bubble wrap, packing peanuts, and packing paper, I will likely need to bump the package into the next weight range. This is why weighing your items in a box similar to what it will ship in is so important. You want to make sure your shipping charges are correct before the item goes for sale on Ebay.

Mentally adding in the packaging material weight is necessary for when packages are close to going to the next pound. For instance, say you have an item in its shipping box with a beginning weight (before packing materials) of 1-pound and 15-ounces. Obviously, when you add in packing materials, the weight will bump up to over 2-pounds and will need to be listed in the 2-3-pound range on Ebay. The same is true if the initial weight is, say, 2-pounds and 13-ounces. When you add in another 3-ounces for packing materials, the weight will be at 3-pounds and will need to be listed in the 3-4-pound range.

So, now that you understand the shipping options and weights, let's set up the **Shipping Details** in an Ebay listing.

The shipping section within an Ebay listing is located about three-quarters of the way down the page under *Shipping Details*. You will be selecting the shipping services first and adding the weight last.

The first section is for **Domestic Shipping.** The drop-down menu lets you choose from four options:

- **Flat:** same cost to all buyers
- **Calculated:** cost varies by buyer location
- **Freight:** large items over 150 lbs.
- **No shipping:** local pickup only

Unless you are shipping a piece of furniture or only offering pickup, you will only need to select the **Flat** OR **Calculated** options before moving on to the next step.

Once you have chosen *Flat* or *Calculated*, you will need to select **Services.** This is where your digital scale comes into play. If you have a lightweight item weighing under one pound (do not forget to add in the 3-ounces for packing material), then you will be able to choose *USPS First Class Package (2 to 5 business days).* However, you can also add in other options under that. I usually offer *USPS Priority Mail (1 to 3 business days)* for the second option. If you want to offer more than one shipping option, just click on *Offer additional service.*

Most of my orders are over 1-pound, so I always offer *USPS Parcel Select Ground (2 to 9 business days)* as my first option since it is promoted as an *Economy Service* and gives the impression that it is the cheapest option available to the buyers. I then offer *USPS Priority Mail (1 to 3 business days)* as the second option for buyers who want to choose an expedited shipping service.

As you will see, when you look at all the shipping options, there are a lot to choose from. I know that looking at all the choices is very overwhelming for new sellers; but just remember to focus on the four I have talked about, which on Ebay are listed:

- **USPS Media Mail (2 to 8 business days)**
- **USPS First Class Package (2 to 5 business days for**

packages a pound or less)
- **USPS Parcel Select (2 to 9 business days for packages over a pound)**
- **USPS Priority Mail (1 to 3 business days for fast delivery of packages over a pound)**

While you may select other options such as *Flat Rate* or *Regional* when you print a label (more on this in the next section), you only need to offer your buyers any one of those options in the actual Ebay listing.

Note that you can choose to offer "free shipping" on your items if you have made sure to build the cost of shipping into the purchase price of your item. If you sell a book that will ship via *Media Mail* for $4, you want to add that $4 to the book's cost. If you list the book for $5 with "free shipping," after the cost of postage and your Ebay fees, you will lose money.

The next choice you need to make is your **Handling time,** which is the number of days it will take you to ship the item after receiving cleared payment. As Ebay points out, buyers like to get their items fast, so I recommend that you choose a handling time between 1 and 3 days.

Because I work from home and utilize *Carrier Pickup*, I offer a handling time of *2 business days.* This means that I ship my items in two BUSINESS DAYS (i.e., weekdays) after a buyer's payment clears. If a buyer pays for their item on a Tuesday, I will ship it out on Wednesday or Thursday. However, if they do not pay until Friday, their item will not ship until Monday.

The next section is for **International shipping.** I recommend just going with **Ebay's Global Shipping Program**, which means you will simply ship any sold items to Ebay's shipping center in Kentucky. From there, they will take care of all customs forms and assume responsibility for shipping the package internationally. Since you will be shipping the item to Ebay's US processing center, the buyer will pay the shipping charges offered under the "Domestic services."

Finally, you are now at the **Package weight & dimensions**, where you will put in the package's weight. First, Ebay has a **Package type** field where you can choose from four options:

- **Letter**
- **Large Envelope**
- **Package (or thick envelope)**
- **Large Package**

If you sell small to mid-size items, you can simply select the **Package (or thick envelope)** option. That is the only option I ever choose. Remember that *Letter* and *Large Envelope* are for flat letter mail; any package, even if in a padded envelope, must go via *Package (or thick envelope)*. Unless you are selling items such as stamps, postcards, or trading cards, your items will all likely ship via *Package (or thick envelope)*.

Next is a field for the **Box dimensions.** Good news: You can completely skip this! The only time you would need to provide a box size up front is if you are shipping an oversized item that will require a box that measures over 36" when you add the length, width, and height together. In that case, you will need to add your box size when you print the item if it is shipping via *Parcel* or *Priority*. You never need to provide the box size for *Media* or *First Class*. Again, stick to boxes that are 12x12x12-inches or less, and you will be fine.

The last field to enter is **Weight**. If you are shipping something that weighs one pound or less, choose the first option, "1 lb. or less," and enter the ounces.

Here is a tip: No matter how many ounces the package weighs, when you are listing the items, enter in 16-ounces. Yes, it will slightly overcharge customers on some packages; but just chalk up any additional funds to your handling fee.

For items weighing a pound or more, simply select the range as I talked about earlier. 1-2 pounds, 2-3 pounds, 3-4 pounds, etc.

Finally, you can **Exclude shipping locations**. Suppose you are shipping internationally on your own and not using Ebay's Global Shipping program. In that case, I strongly advise blocking buyers in some regions of the world prone to fraud and missing packages. Known trouble spots are all of Africa and the Middle East, as well as Italy. Most international buyers on Ebay are from Canada, the United Kingdom, and Australia anyway, and they are all safe places to ship to. However, where to sell to is entirely up to you. If you are nervous about shipping internationally at all, even through *Global Shipping*, stick to domestic shipments until you feel more confident.

The next step to completing your listing is to click on the **List item** button at the bottom of the page, which will make your listing live and for sale on Ebay's site. However, you can first **Preview** the listing to see what it will look like when live; you can also **Save as draft** if you still need to add some details to it.

After submitting a listing, I like to open it up to review what it actually looks like on the site. Sometimes I can quickly catch a mistake I may have made in the title or on a photo. I also utilize the "share" buttons located within each live Ebay listing to share it out to Facebook, Twitter, and Pinterest.

And that is all there is to shipping! If you are still feeling overwhelmed, trust me when I tell you that shipping will become as routine to you as brushing your teeth once you have a few orders under your belt. It honestly only takes shipping a handful of packages for you to become a pro!

CHAPTER NINE:

PROCESSING ORDERS

Finally, the most exciting part of selling on Ebay has arrived: You have SOLD something! Now it is time to print your label and package up the order.

Ebay will notify you via email when you have made a sale, so be sure to check your email regularly when you have items listed. If you are using the **Ebay App**, you can also set up notifications to be delivered to your cell phone whenever you make a sale.

In your **Seller Hub**, click on the **Orders** tab at the top of the page. Here is where Ebay provides you with the following under the **Manage All Orders** column:

- Awaiting payment
- Awaiting shipment
- Paid and shipped
- Cancellations
- Returns
- Cases
- Shipping labels
- Archived
- Return preferences

Keeping the page on the **All orders** setting, you will notice that within each section for every item there is a tiny down arrow that opens a drop-down menu. Here you will find numerous options:

- Print shipping label
- Cancel order
- View payment details
- Add/edit note
- Relist
- Sell similar
- Contact buyer
- Report buyer
- Send refund
- View order details
- Archive

If the buyer has yet to pay for their item, you will also see a **Send an Invoice** option. Note that some buyers WANT you to send them an invoice after buying an item, even though the shipping options are already set up for them. Fortunately, a quick click sends an invoice, so be prepared to do that occasionally. And you will also need to send an invoice to anyone who buys two or more items from you to combine shipping for them.

I have my *Fixed Price* listings set so that buyers must pay immediately. However, buyers obviously cannot pay immediately when they are bidding on items through an *Auction*, so you will likely have to send invoices to auction winners.

If you have chosen to sell internationally using Ebay's *Global Shipping Program,* Ebay will handle the invoicing for you. So, if someone in the United Kingdom buys an item from you, you will not be able to invoice them. Ebay will do it on their end as they will be figuring out the shipping as the customer will pay you the cost to send the item to Ebay's *Global Shipping* center, and then they will also pay Ebay to ship that item overseas.

Ebay requires that sellers give buyers at least two days to pay for their purchases. After that, you can open an **Unpaid Item Case,** after which the buyer has four additional days to pay. If, after those four days, they still have not paid, you can close the case. Ebay will refund you your selling fees and, if you want, relist the item for you.

If I do not have immediate payment required on an item and someone buys it but does not pay within an hour or so, I send them an invoice. Then the next day, I send a "friendly" reminder that their payment is due by the following business day. If they still do not pay, I open a case. Opening a case usually prompts buyers to pay, but sometimes they do not. And while it is frustrating to have someone not pay for an item, in the end, there is nothing you can do except eventually close the case, relist the item, and add the buyer to your **Blocked Bidders List.** Most Ebay customers do, however, pay for their orders promptly.

Once a customer pays for their item, it is time to print out the shipping label. The default selection in the drop-down menu next to the item will be to **Print Shipping Label.** All you need to do is click on that link, and you will be taken to Ebay's **Print your shipping label** screen. Please note that sometimes you may have to log in a second time here due to Ebay's tight security settings.

The Ebay label printing screen has **Print your shipping label** at the top, along with the **Order details.** Listed here will be the **Ship to address** for the buyer as well as the **Ship from/Return to (your) address**. You only must choose **Print format** once; Ebay will remember it for the next time you go to ship an order. I have my settings at *PDF 8" x 11"* as I print on two-to-a-sheet mailing labels. Here is where you can also preview what the shipping label will look like.

You will also see the item that sold, which is clickable and will take you to a copy of the listing. And you will see the buyer's Ebay screen name, the shipping service they selected (or that you chose for them when you set up the listing), the order value, the delivery charge, and the expected date of delivery.

In the middle of the screen is the section called **Package.** This is where new Ebay sellers typically get tripped up, so take a breath as we go through it. After you have shipped out a few packages, I promise that this will become a routine step for you in no time!

Since you set up your shipping preferences when you created your listing, the selections here will match those from the listing. Let's say you are shipping that Ralph Lauren shirt we used as an example earlier in this book. It weighs under a pound, so you listed the shipping option as *USPS First Class*. That option will automatically be selected for you under the *Service* section of the page.

However, let's say that you offered *Flat Rate* shipping of $5.99 for the shirt, which the buyer paid. When you put the shirt into a poly mailer and weighed it, the weight came to ten ounces. While you can ship via *First Class* for items one pound or less, the price differs by ounces. **The ounce parameters for First Class packages are:**

- **1 to 4 ounces**
- **5 to 8 ounces**
- **9 to 12 ounces**
- **13 to 16 ounces**

Your shirt can ship in the 9–12-ounce range, which means not only will the $5.99 shipping cost cover your postage, it will also give you a bit of extra money to put toward shipping supplies. Think of these types of overages as your handling fee.

For the shirt, I would typically just type 12-ounces into the **Weight** field. Since the cost is the same in the 9-12 range, I do not have to enter the exact ten ounces. However, the weight will show up on the label, so I like to put in a higher amount.

Next to *Weight* is **Dimensions.** I usually leave this at the default of 1x1x1 until it is time to ship an item, as I am never quite sure what envelope or box I will be using. However, unless you are shipping something larger than 12x12x12, you can put whatever dimensions you want here. Sometimes when I list an item, I will just enter 10x10x10, and that size will then show up on the shipping label page. The main point here is to show that you are shipping something UNDER what USPS considers oversized. If I were shipping something in a 14x14x14 box, I would need to put in those measurements as they will affect the package options and shipping costs available.

But, back to the shirt. You have changed the *Weight* to ten ounces, you have left the *Dimensions* at their default of 1x1x1, and *USPS First Class Package* has been automatically selected under *Service*. There are some **Additional Options** available to you, including:

- Require Signature at delivery (use this only for items of high value)
- Add additional liability coverage (this is added insurance; only buy this if your item is valued over $100)
- Contains hazardous materials (click on the link next to this option to see all the restricted items)
- Display postage value on label (I make sure this is NOT checked so that the buyer does not see that they may have paid a bit more for shipping)
- Add custom text on label (this is if you want to add an inventory number)
- Add a message in the dispatch confirmation email

I leave all these options unchecked. In fact, I rarely even notice them! Underneath these options is **Select how to pay**, and if you are in *Ebay's Managed Payments,* the cost of the label will be taken out of your pending payouts.

And finally, you will see the total cost of postage next to the **big blue button titled Purchase and print label.** By clicking on that, your Ebay shipping label will print!

Let's go back and change the example of the item you have sold from a shirt to a coffee mug. While you listed the shirt with *Flat Rate Shipping* of $5.99, the coffee mug weighs over a pound when packaged in a shipping box. Therefore, you cannot send it via *USPS First Class*. In fact, the cost to ship the mug will vary widely depending on the buyer's location.

I live in Iowa, and for packages over one pound that ship to California, the postage cost is nearly $11. However, the same package can ship to Minnesota for around $8. And with the Post Office continually raising the postage cost, the shipping charges keep going up and up. That is why it is so important to use *Calculated Shipping* on orders that weigh over one pound UNLESS the item can ship in a *Flat Rate* box.

The USPS offers several sizes and types of *Priority Flat Rate* envelopes and boxes, including *Regional Rate* options. The most popular *Flat Rate* option for resellers is the *Priority Mail Flat Rate Bubble Mailer* as many non-breakable items, such as jackets and other bulky yet soft things, can be stuffed into the envelopes for a reasonable rate. The wide variety of shipping options is why I like to offer my customers the slowest, cheapest rate possible and examine all the choices before paying for postage.

If you are using a *USPS Priority Mail FLAT RATE box*, select **Carrier packages** to choose which box or envelope you are using. You do not have to enter weight or dimension if you are shipping in a *Flat Rate* box or envelope, including *Regional Rate* boxes.

For instance, let's reexamine that coffee mug. You initially listed it in the 1-2-pound range with *Parcel Select* as the default option. However, once you are in the Print your shipping label section, look at all the options available. Depending on where the buyer lives, the price could go up or down between *Parcel* and *Priority,* or you may see that using a *Flat Rate* box will be cheaper.

Let's say that you can ship the mug cheapest via *Priority*. That means you can ship the mug in a free *Priority Mail* box, and the buyer will get it faster than if it were going *Parcel Select*, and you will profit a small handling fee from the excess. Plus, the customer will be happy that they received their order well before the promised delivery.

However, you may find that *Parcel Select* IS the best price, so you can just stick with that. When you shop online, you get FREE tracking with *First Class, Parcel,* and *Priority* (*Media Mail* tracking has a small fee). You will also notice a discount on *First Class* and *Priority* shipping for printing the labels online. Free tracking and discount postage are two of the best reasons for shipping online!

Once your shipping label prints, the postage and the fees associated with the sale will be taken from your Ebay pending balance account. The cost for the label is paid directly to the USPS within Ebay's system. So once the label is printed, all your Ebay fees and postage costs related to that order have been paid; you do not owe any more money to Ebay or USPS regarding that order. You will, however, still have a charge on your account for your Ebay Store subscription if you have one.

After you print your label, you also have the option of printing a packing slip. Simply click on **Open packing slip** if you would like to print one. I always include a packing slip in my orders, but not all sellers do. Again, the decision is yours to make.

Packing Your Orders: Once your label has been printed, both you and the buyer will receive a notice from Ebay that the package has shipped. The tracking information will be included in this notice, and it will also be uploaded onto the item transaction page for both you and your buyer to access on your respective My Ebay pages. This is a wonderful feature as you, your customer, and Ebay now have confirmation from the USPS that the label has been printed. You do not have to type in tracking manually, and if there are any issues with a lost package, you will be able to quickly show that you indeed did ship the item out.

Now that you have your label printed, all that is left to do is seal your package and attach the label to it! Since you weighed the item in the box or envelope you planned to ship it in before you ever listed it, you will now want to go ahead and start packaging the item for shipment.

Even when selling used items and using secondhand packing materials, it is still essential to take time to package up your items in a clean and professional manner. I keep all sorts of packaging materials on hand, everything from recycled packing paper to bubble wrap. As you are just starting out, try and use items from shipments you have gotten. If you do not have anything around, ask friends and family for any boxes, bubble wrap, and packing peanuts they may have.

If you are just going to sell on Ebay occasionally, you might be able to get most of your shipping supplies for free by reusing what you have or asking for people to give you their leftovers. However, it is important that whatever you use is CLEAN and from SMOKE-FREE HOMES! If you are a smoker, be sure to keep your inventory AND your packing supplies in an area away from the smoke. If your buyer detects even the slightest scent of cigarettes, they WILL complain!

Using a combination of packing paper, bubble wrap, and/or packing peanuts, carefully wrap the item and make sure it is surrounded by a buffer of packaging material in the box. I use newspapers to create a barrier around the item and the box sides, but

I always make sure the item itself is wrapped in paper or bubble wrap away from the newsprint to prevent any print from rubbing off on the item.

If you are printing your shipping labels onto actual peel-and-stick labels, you will just need to remove the backing and stick the label to the package. However, if you are printing your labels onto paper, you will need to use clear packing tape to adhere the label to the outside of the box. It usually takes me three small pieces to cover the label and make sure it is stuck tightly. The only part of the label that I do NOT cover with tape is the bar code. You want to leave the bar code free of the tape so that the Post Office's scanning equipment can easily read it.

Once your label is affixed to your package, it is ready to be shipped out! If you are at home and can arrange for pickup, you will want to take advantage of the FREE *Carrier Pickup* service. If you have at least one *Priority Mail* package, your postal carrier will pick up all your packages for free. You do need to request package pick up the night before, however.

If you cannot be home for *Carrier Pickup* and need to take your packages to the Post Office, note that you will likely have to stand in line and hand them to a clerk. If you end up shipping out many packages and developing a good relationship with the clerks, they may allow you to leave your packages on the counter. If you do hand them directly to a clerk, they can scan them and give you a receipt. I usually skip this since I have the tracking information from Ebay loaded onto my account.

And that is it! Your order is packaged and ready to be shipped off to the buyer. Ebay will notify the buyer that their order has shipped, providing both them and you with the tracking number. Both you and the buyer can then track the progress of the shipment. Note that the tracking numbers for each order are easily accessible next to the item itself in your *Seller Hub* list of orders that have shipped. Most buyers know how to access the tracking number, although new Ebay users may not. So, it is not uncommon for buyers to ask you directly for the number.

CHAPTER TEN:

MARKETING & PROMOTION

When I first started selling online, Ebay and Amazon were the only two e-commerce retailers. Customers who shopped online only had those two sites to choose from, so there was no need for sellers to seek out buyers. However, nowadays, it is often not enough to simply list an item on Ebay for it to sell; you now must do some promotion and marketing to drive sales, both on the Ebay site directly as well as on social media platforms, to compete with the thousands of other e-commerce sites out there.

Fortunately, most of these promotional tools are free and easy to use, especially when it comes to utilizing social media sites to promote your Ebay listings. By adding some or all the following marketing methods, you will see your Ebay traffic and sales increase. In some cases, you may need to spend a little bit of money (such as if you decide to set up a website and/or have enclosures printed up); but even then, the costs are still relatively low compared to the huge differences these efforts can make for your sales.

Blog/Website: If Ebay is your part-time or full-time business, it may be worth it to you to set up a blog or even a full-fledged website to further connect with customers. If you are going to have a site, however, be sure to commit to maintaining it. Nothing is worse than going to someone's blog and seeing that they have not updated it in months.

However, if you are only selling on Ebay occasionally or just for a bit of extra money, then you do not need to burden yourself with the work of maintaining a site. Ask yourself the following questions:

- Do you plan to write lengthy articles discussing the items you sell?
- Are you looking to use your site not just as a sales channel but also as a teaching tool?
- Would you like to sell products directly from your website outside of Ebay, or are you selling your items on other online sites (Amazon, Etsy) and/or at brick-and-mortar retail locations (your own shop or at an antique mall)?
- Would you like to explore affiliate advertising and/or sell advertising to earn extra money for your site?

If you answered "yes" to any of the above questions, then you may want to consider starting a site. However, you will need to decide whether to go with a free blogging platform or a paid website. If you decide to go the paid route, you can invest in a sophisticated system or choose a simple, low-cost one. Yes, there are lots of decisions to make!

Both Blogger and WordPress offer free blogging platforms. Note that Google owns Blogger; therefore, you can apply for a Google AdSense account and place ads on your blog. So not only will you be helping drive traffic to your Ebay listings to increase sales, but you will also be able to earn advertising revenue.

However, if you decide to go with a paid website, do your research as there are a lot out there to choose from. If your main business is selling on Ebay, you want your *Ebay Store* to be your brand, with your blog/website acting as an additional tool to drive traffic to your listings. There are a lot of low-cost website options out there. For instance, you can not only register for the website URLs on GoDaddy.com, but they also offer website inexpensive hosting and simple websites.

If you sell on other websites in addition to Ebay, a blog/website is a great place to provide the links to those places (Amazon, Etsy, flea markets, and/or antique malls). In addition to posting about new inventory and sales, you can include photos and talk about what is going on behind the scenes with your business. Having a site gives people a more personal look as to who you are. Also, it confirms that you are running a legitimate business, both of which can go a long way toward building up trust and reassuring people that they can buy from you with confidence.

Note that in addition to posting updates on your blog, you will need to maintain it. If you allow visitors to leave comments on your posts, you will want to make sure to respond to them. You also want to make sure all links are active and up-to-date so that people do not click through and get an error.

Suppose you are selling a significant number of items on Ebay and plan to continue with it as your primary business. In that case, you may want to register for a domain name, i.e., a personal website address that matches your Ebay Store name. For years, I have maintained a URL of my Ebay Store name that sends people directly to my Ebay Store. Having a URL gives you an easy web address to share with customers that is shorter and easier to remember. You can purchase domain names on a website like GoDaddy.com.

You will also have to decide *where* you want the URL to direct users to. Do you want people to go to your blog FIRST, or do you want them to always go to your Ebay Store? Remember, you should be using a blog/website to *complement* your Ebay Store, not as a replacement. If you decide to go with a free blog on a site like Blogger, you may want to choose a URL that sends people directly to your Ebay Store (i.e., www.MyStore.com) and keep the URL you get from Blogger for your website as-is. Or choose another URL such as MyEbayStoreBlog.com just for your site.

My advice is to have a personalized URL address that points to your Ebay Store, as getting Ebay sales should always be your priority. Your website should work to direct traffic to your Ebay listings, not to intercept them.

Mailing List: When I sold new gift items, I tended to get a lot of repeat customers. I developed my own email mailing list using the PayPal email address that I had access to once someone paid me. I simply copied and pasted email addresses into a Word document and then put them into the *Blind Carbon Copy* section of my email program when I wanted to send out a message.

However, with Ebay's *Managed Payments*, sellers no longer have access to customer emails. If you sell a lot of similar items, you can always create your own mailing list by using a service such as Constant Contact or Mail Chimp and letting customers know that they can sign up for the list in an enclosure card included in their order. Note that it is against Ebay's policy for you to use their messaging system to direct people off their site, so if you want to cultivate a mailing list, be sure to do so off the Ebay system.

Again, I would only consider a mailing list if you sell similar types of items. If, like most resellers, you have a wide variety of different items for sale on Ebay, I would skip the mailing list and instead focus on creating listings that will show up high in internet search rankings (keyword-loaded titles, good photos, and accurate descriptions).

Facebook: If you plan to be selling a lot of items on Ebay, it is worth your time to set up a Facebook page to promote your listings. Some sellers choose to make their personal Facebook page their business page, too. Still, suppose you are already actively participating on Facebook by using your personal page to communicate with your friends and family. In that case, I recommend that you set up a separate business page. A personal page is one where people add you as a "friend," while a business page is one people must "like."

I prefer the business page format for promoting Ebay listings because it keeps your personal life and business separate. There is a limit to how many "friends" you can accept to a personal page, but you can grow an unlimited number of business "fans" on a business page. However, to start a business page, you need first to have a personal page.

To set up a Facebook business page, simply visit **facebook.com/about/pages.** You will need to log into your personal Facebook account first, and then the system will walk you through the steps needed to create your business page. It is FREE and easy to set up.

The first decision you will need to make is to name your page. I currently have three Facebook business pages: one for my Ebay Store, one for my own name (to promote my books and videos), and one for my stationery brand. If you are starting your Facebook page specifically for your Ebay business, then you will want to make the names match.

In fact, as you go forward with creating more social media accounts related to your Ebay business, you will want to make sure they all have the same name. Now is the time to evaluate your Facebook user name to make sure it matches your Ebay Store and is a good name overall. For instance, if you have been using the Ebay user name "i_luv_cats," you may want to change it to something more professional.

To change your Ebay user name, simply go to **My eBay** and then **Account**. Click **Personal Information** on the left side of the page. **Then** click **Edit** to the right of the information you want to change.

To change the name of your Ebay Store, simply go to **My eBay**, **Account**, and then **Subscriptions**. On the **Manage My Store: Summary** page, scroll to the **Set Up, Sell and Track** section and click the **Design Your Store** link. In the **Display Settings** section, click the **Change** link and make your edits.

Once you have gotten your Ebay user name and Ebay Store name straight, you can proceed with naming your Facebook page the same.

There are all kinds of things you can personalize on your Facebook page. You can add a profile picture and a banner. I have my logo as my profile picture, and I had a custom banner made on Fiverr.com, although you can also design your own graphics using sites such as Canva and apps such as WordSwag. Whatever photos or graphics you choose, remember that this is your BUSINESS page, so keep it professional.

You will also want to fill out the extensive **About** section to provide people with information about your page and business. However, since this is your BUSINESS page and separate from your personal page, you want to be careful with how much information you provide. While you may share your cell phone number on your personal page so that friends and family can call or text you, unless you have a brick-and-mortar location that you want people to call, you will want to leave that section blank on your business page.

You will first need to choose the **Category** for your page; as an Ebay seller, there are several you can choose from, such as "Companies & Organizations," "Local Businesses," or "Websites & Blogs." Any of the three would be sufficient for your Ebay page; it is up to you which you prefer. You will need to select a sub-category, too. And don't worry about being locked into your selections; you can easily change them at any time.

In addition to your **Name** (the name of your page, i.e., your Ebay business name), you can edit your Facebook URL so that it ends in that name, too.

The **About** section has fields for both a **Short Description** and a **Long Description**. I have my tagline in the *Short* section and a much more detailed account of what I do in the *Long* section.

Since you provided information about you and your business in the *Short* and *Long* description sections, use the **General Information** field to share the links to your other social media sites. You will want to **put the address to your Ebay Store in the main Website field** (remember, your main goal is to drive traffic to your Ebay listings), but add any other links you may have (blog/website, Twitter, Pinterest, Instagram, etc.) to the *General Information* section so that users can easily connect with you on all your social media platforms.

One great feature you can add to your Facebook page is a **Shop Now** tab that will take users directly to your Ebay Store. Simply click on **More** at the top of the page and select **Manage Tabs** to add a **Call to Action – Shop Now** button. Link it to your Ebay Store to create an easy way for your Facebook fans to shop your Ebay listings.

Finally, at the top of the page, click on **Settings** to determine how users can interact with you. I have stringent privacy settings for my page. I do not allow people to message me or post on my wall. When I had these two features turned off, I was inundated with messages and posts. However, if having messages from people is okay with you, then, by all means, leave those options open. You can always change them later.

Once you have your page set up, it is time to start building your audience by getting people to "Like" your page. You will be able to invite friends and family on your personal page to "Like" your new business page. If you are a part of Ebay groups, you can also post about your new page and hope that fellow Ebayers will support you.

To bring customers (past, present, or potential) to your Facebook page, include the link to your page on any package enclosures. I have business card sized "thank you" notes that go into every order printed with the direct link to my Ebay Store as well as the links to my blog and social media accounts.

So, you have set up a Facebook page for your business and have started getting people to "Like" it. Now what? Providing helpful content on your page will be vital to keeping it up to date and attracting new followers.

I share my newest listings directly to my Facebook page as Ebay makes this incredibly easy to do. In the upper right-hand corner of all active Ebay listings are **social media "Share" icons** for *Facebook, Twitter, Pinterest,* and *Email.* Simply click on the **Facebook icon**, change the page you want to post to (it will show you your personal page and business page, so be sure to select your business page), type in something like "Just Listed!" or "On Sale!," and then hit "Share." In only a few seconds, many of the people who have "Liked" your page will now have your listing on their Facebook feed!

In addition to sharing listings, it is also a good idea to engage your Facebook fans by posting status updates about what is going on with your business, such as if you are getting in new inventory or if you are running a sale. You want to keep your business page postings POSITIVE; stay away from religious, political, or other controversial topics. Remember, your goal with Ebay is to make money, and you cannot do that by offending people. Save the personal commentary for your personal Facebook page.

Posting pictures of your office, new inventory, or even a shot of orders ready to ship out are all fun ways to keep your audience interested. And sharing unique content is vital to ensure people actually see your posts.

Facebook makes it increasingly difficult for people to see all content on their feeds as Facebook wants page owners to purchase advertising. You may have noticed a little "Boost" link under your posts. "Boosting" a post means that you must PAY for Facebook to show it to people. Pricing for this starts at $5; the more you pay, the more people Facebook will show your ad to.

If your sales are slow, it can be tempting to start boosting all your posts to drive traffic to your Ebay listings. And while it can be advantageous to spend $5 here and there to help people see your content, do not let yourself become consumed if every post does not reach a broad audience. Likely, the links you share of your listings will not be shown to as many people as photos you post directly to your page (i.e., unique content).

As I mentioned earlier, you may decide that a Facebook page can act like your blog or website rather than setting up a separate site. Many Ebay sellers do not have a blog or website; instead, they use their Facebook page as their business homepage. So, unless you have the time to devote to maintaining a separate website, consider just using Facebook along with other social networking to promote your Ebay business. I recommend you do Facebook first, as you can always add a blog/website later as you grow your business.

Facebook is just the first in a long list of social media sites you can create in conjunction with your Ebay business. Master your Facebook page first before moving on to the next social media account: Twitter!

Twitter: If you do not already have a Twitter account, you can create one for FREE at Twitter.com. If you do have an account that you are active on, consider creating a new one just for your Ebay business. As with Facebook, you want to keep your personal and business lives separate on Twitter. Make sure your Twitter handle is the same as your Ebay user name, Ebay Store name, and Facebook business page name.

Twitter allows users to share posts of 280 characters or less. And just like Facebook, Twitter is a fast, easy, and free way to promote your listings. As with sharing your listings to Facebook, Ebay makes it easy to share your Twitter listings using the share button located in all active Ebay listings (in the upper right-hand corner).

To share a listing via Twitter, first, you will want to copy the title of your listing to your clipboard (simply highlight and select "copy"). Ebay and Twitter often have a generic "check out what I found on Ebay" title already in place when you click on the Twitter share button, so you will want to replace that with your keyword-loaded title. Simply delete the text in the Tweet that you want to replace and paste in your title.

Adding in hashtags is another easy way to make sure potential customers see your Tweet. A hashtag is a pound (#) sign followed by a keyword, and it is what experienced Twitter users enter in the search field to seek out relevant Tweets. For example, let's say your Ebay listing title is "Red Mens Polo RALPH LAUREN Dress Shirt LARGE Pony Logo Stretch." Put that into a new Twitter "tweet," followed by the link to the listing. And after the link, add in hashtags such as #RalphLauren #Polo #MensClothing.

Just as you share your Facebook page with customers via a blog/website and/or package enclosures (as I have said, I include business card sized "thank you" notes in all my Ebay packages with my Ebay Store link as well as all my social media URL's), you will also want to share your Twitter handle with them in the hopes they will follow you on Twitter, too. And to find even more followers, you want to engage with other Twitter users actively.

Some Twitter users follow everyone who follows them, which can certainly help build up your followers. You can also "network" with other folks on Twitter by replying to, retweeting, or favoring tweets. As I mentioned when setting up your Facebook page, you can add all your social media links, including your Twitter URL, in the "About" section; so hopefully, some of your Facebook fans will follow you to Twitter. To encourage this, about once a week, post your Twitter link directly to your Facebook page to make it easy for people to click through and "follow" you.

What you want to gain from Twitter is people clicking through to your Ebay listing links and either purchasing that item or finding something else to buy from you. You will also likely see that some people "favor" your Tweets by clicking on the little star icon under each message. It is always nice when someone retweets one of your Tweets, too, so that it gets shared with their followers.

Note that just as people can message you on Facebook (unless you change the privacy settings to block them), you can also send and receive messages on Twitter. And finally, you can create "Lists" on Twitter to group people you follow together (such as "customers," "Ebay sellers," "celebrities," "news," etc.).

Pinterest: Pinterest started as a way for people, mainly women, to "pin" craft ideas and recipes to virtual boards. However, Pinterest is quickly becoming a tool for businesses to get the word out about their products and develop brand loyalty. Pinterest offers Ebay sellers another fast and free way to promote their listings in the hopes that people will click through and purchase products.

As with Facebook and Twitter, Ebay provides a Pinterest "share" button in all active listings (in the upper right-hand corner). I have a "For Sale on Ebay" board on Pinterest that I "pin" my listings to. Not only can my Pinterest followers then see my new listings, but they can share the pin with THEIR Pinterest followers by pinning it to their own boards.

You will find many other Ebay sellers on Pinterest, many of whom have created Ebay group boards that you may be invited to post to. Networking with fellow Ebay sellers on Pinterest is another excellent way to promote your listings while getting to know other Ebayers such as yourself. Re-pinning THEIR pins is a nice gesture and a great way to network.

One concern many Ebay sellers have is that once items sell, the "pin" is no longer relevant. Should you delete old pins of items that have sold? While you certainly can take the time to do this, you do not have to. In fact, it may be beneficial for you to leave the pin active. Why? Well, let's say someone sees a pin of a collectible you have for sale. When they click through, they find that the item has sold. However, they are now connected with you on Ebay and may click on the link to visit your Ebay Store or to see your current listings. While they may be annoyed that the item they wanted is no longer available, they also might find something else to buy from you.

Just as you should be doing with your Facebook and Twitter links, be sure to share your Pinterest page with customers by including the link on your blog/website (if you have one) and in the General Information section of your Facebook page. You can also provide the URL to your Pinterest account in any package enclosures. Be sure to periodically share your Pinterest link on both Facebook and Twitter in order to attract new followers.

You may be noticing by now that a big part of social networking is to have all your sites working together. Include all your social media links on your blog/website and in package enclosures. Post your Twitter and Pinterest links to Facebook; share your Facebook and Pinterest links on Twitter. The more you can get your Ebay links out there, the easier it will be for customers to find you and for you to make more sales and make more money!

Instagram: Like Facebook, Twitter, and Pinterest, Instagram is easy and FREE to use. While Ebay does not yet provide a "share" button for Instagram, it is still a valuable tool for promoting your listings. You can currently only add photos to your Instagram through their apps, so note that you will need to have a phone or tablet to use the site.

In addition to helping to drive traffic to your Ebay Store, Instagram is also great for connecting with customers on a personal level by sharing photos that may not always relate directly to your business. However, as with anything you share on your business accounts, be sure to keep Instagram pictures non-controversial and lighthearted (i.e., avoid politics and religion!). Take photos of your office or of all the packages you are shipping out. Include pictures of your pets and even what you are having for lunch. Make it your goal to post at least one photo to Instagram every day.

Hashtags are a big part of getting your content on Instagram found. I like to include at least five with every photo I share. The goal of these hashtags is that people will search for them and find me.

When I post a photo related to Ebay, I use hashtags such as:

- #ebay
- #ebayer
- #reseller
- #reselling
- #picker
- #thrifting
- #workfromhome
- #selfemployed

Instagram allows you to include one website link in your profile;

so, if you are using Instagram to bring in Ebay customers, you will want to make that the link to your Ebay Store. And while you can include the link when you share a photo, it will not be active. Therefore, a tip is to put something like, "25% off sale going on right now in our Ebay Store; direct link in profile @yourinstagramaccount." The "@" link will take users to your profile page, where the active link to your Ebay Store will be. Then the user simply clicks on your Ebay Store URL, taking them straight to your Ebay listings.

Some sellers are also using Instagram to sell items directly, skipping Ebay altogether. Many sellers will put up a picture of an item and offer it up for sale right on Instagram. All someone must do is message the poster (Instagram has a "mailbox" system that allows users to message one another) to give them their email so the seller can send them a PayPal invoice.

Just like with Facebook, Twitter, and Pinterest, you will want to network with other Ebay sellers and even your customers by following them back on Instagram and "liking" their posts. Include the link to your Instagram page on your blog/website, package enclosures, and Facebook page. And share your Instagram link periodically on Facebook and Twitter.

TikTok: TikTok is the newest entry into the social media world and is promoted as a video-sharing social network. The TikTok app allows users to create short-form mobile videos. The platform has a vast catalog of sounds and song clips along with special effects and filters. Other users can "react" to TikToks, allowing them to record their reactions in side-by-side frames to other creators' content. TikTok is growing by the day as more users, particularly celebrities, join the app.

As with any fast-growing platform, businesses are jumping on the TikTok bandwagon, too; and as an Ebay seller, you can also leverage it to drive traffic to your listings. Creating a TikTok account and putting the link to your Ebay Store in your profile can potentially attract customers by showing off newly listed items.

YouTube: A blog/website. Facebook. Twitter. Pinterest. Instagram. TikTok. Are you feeling overwhelmed? Take a deep breath and relax; no one expects you to master these social networking sites and techniques in one day. Take one at a time before moving on to the next one. Once you have mastered the second site, continue to the third, and so on.

We have already covered the biggest sites Ebay sellers are using to drive sales and make more money, but there are still others you can use, including YouTube. Not only can you use YouTube to drive traffic to your Ebay listings, but you can also make money on your videos through Google's AdSense program.

But what kind of videos can you make that will help you increase your Ebay sales? One way to use YouTube to help sell your Ebay items is to take videos of products you have listed and include those videos in your Ebay listings. And you can also share the video via your other social media accounts, hoping that viewers will click through to the actual listing.

Note that making videos can be time-consuming, so shooting a video for every single item you have listed would likely not be worth it, especially for lower-priced items. However, for items you are selling that have moving parts, play music, or are higher priced, adding a video to the listing may help sell it.

Under every YouTube video is a description box where you can include information as well as links. I include the links to my *Amazon Author Page,* blog, and all social media accounts, plus my Ebay Store under my videos so that viewers can easily click on the links to visit my various sites.

What many Ebay sellers do to grow their sales via YouTube is to make videos showing new inventory they will be listing. I do haul videos on my YouTube channel showing all the items I picked up at estate sales and thrift stores that I will be selling on Ebay. Not only does this help educate others about how they can make money on Ebay, but it also lets customers know what items will be showing up in my Ebay Store soon.

However, more than driving sales, making videos about your Ebay business is about connecting with other sellers. Selling on Ebay can be a bit lonely when you do not know anyone else who does it. And chances are your friends and family do not understand what you do (or they just want you to sell their stuff for them). By sharing your Ebay business through YouTube videos and by searching out others, you will quickly find yourself networking will fellow resellers. And once you connect on YouTube, you can also connect on Facebook, Twitter, and other social networks.

You may think Ebay sellers compete with one another, but I have found the opposite to be true. People who sell on Ebay love meeting others who do, too. They enjoy watching YouTube videos about selling on Ebay, and they support each other on social networking.

And if you, like me, source secondhand items to resell on Ebay (from thrift stores, garage sales, and estate sales), YouTube is a fantastic resource to learn what items to look for to make money. When I transitioned from selling new gift items to secondhand goods, YouTube videos helped teach me what items to look for when I was out "picking."

You do not need a fancy camera or high-price editing software to make YouTube videos. I film mine on an iPhone! After you upload a video, you can monetize it so that it brings in AdSense revenue. And once your video goes live, you can share it to social media via the convenient "share" icons YouTube provides under each video.

I make all kinds of Ebay related videos, including the hauls I mentioned earlier. I have also filmed many how-to videos teaching people everything from how to list items to what shipping materials I use.

LinkedIn: LinkedIn is a social networking site specifically for the business community. Rather than sharing family photos as you do on Facebook, you want to keep LinkedIn strictly professional by only sharing your business content such as blog posts and Tweets related to your Ebay business.

Creating a LinkedIn account is free and easy, and you can automatically connect your account with your other social networking sites. As with Facebook, LinkedIn allows you to connect with fellow users. You can search out friends and past co-workers. Think of LinkedIn as an online resume where you highlight your past accomplishments and share your current business activities.

Does my LinkedIn activity bring me any Ebay customers? Not really. However, since it is free to create an account, it is something you should take the time to do to add to your social media presence. There are Ebay seller groups on LinkedIn that you may want to check out, too. And if you are open to selling on consignment, LinkedIn could be a way to find clients.

Putting It All Together: When you sell on Ebay, your primary concern should be creating new Ebay listings, sourcing new inventory, answering customer questions, and shipping out orders. A good title, photos, and description are crucial to creating an Ebay listing that will result in a sale. Think of social media as the final step in that listing creation process.

As I have mentioned several times before, Ebay makes it easy to share your listings to Facebook, Twitter, and Pinterest via "share" buttons located in every active listing. After I finish creating a listing, I click on the active link and go to the upper right-hand side of the page where the "share" buttons are. I click through to each one and post my listings to the respective sites. Note that connecting your Ebay account to your social media networks is a one-time step; once you have set up the connections, they will remain linked. It only takes about 15 seconds for me to share a listing out to the three main social media sites, a little longer if I add in hashtags.

One tip is that if you are listing a large batch of items, share each individually to Twitter and Pinterest but hold off on Facebook. Why? I talked before about how Facebook likes to "hide" business page posts, only showing your page followers a limited number of posts. So, if you flood Facebook with link after link, Facebook will hide most of them from your followers' feeds.

Instead, wait until you have finished listing for the day and then post a photo of the items you listed to Facebook with a link to your Ebay Store. I like to use an app for creating photo collages to make one photo showing several items. Facebook tends to show individual photos over direct links, so it is much more likely followers will see the one photo you post and click through to your listings through it.

If you are using Instagram, try posting a photo at least a few times a week, if not daily. You can upload shots of your office, new inventory, or even what you are having for lunch. Include three to five hashtags so that users can find you. And be sure you are following other users and "liking" their content, too. I like to spend a few minutes scrolling through my Instagram feed to connect with other users at the end of the day.

Having a blog/website and/or YouTube channel will add a considerable amount of more work for you, so only use them if you feel they are benefitting your sales or you are getting something from them personally (as in networking with other sellers). If you do utilize those options, be sure to share the content you create over to all your other social networking sites.

When I upload a new YouTube video, I share it with Facebook, Twitter, and Pinterest using the "share" buttons under the video. I also manually share the link to the video on Instagram and TikTok..

While I put in a lot of effort to market my Ebay Store online, I also have promotional tools I use offline. As I mentioned earlier, I include a packing slip in all my Ebay orders (you can print these directly from Ebay after your shipping label has been printed); and I also include a business card sized "thank you" note in all packages (I order these from VistaPrint). The cards contain my Ebay Store URL in the hope customers will come back to shop with me. It also gives orders a personal touch that helps cultivate positive feedback.

Ebay's Own Marketing Tools: While the various social media sites help advertise your Ebay business, you can also utilize several features directly through Ebay to drive sales.

In the **Seller Hub**, click on the **Marketing tab** at the top of the page. Here you will be able to access:

- **Branding for your Ebay Store**
- **Promotions**
- **Markdown sale**
- **Advertising via Promoted Listings**

Clicking on the **Store** link will take you to a page where you can edit your Ebay Store information, including your:

- **Store name** (you can change your store name at any time)
- **Billboard** (an image that expresses your brand, shows your products, or announces a promotion or event; also referred to as a "banner")
- **Logo** (300px x 300pm and 12MB max file size)

- **Description** (a short blurb about you and what you sell; it will appear when buyers search for your store on Ebay)
- **Featured Listings** (great if you sell multi-quantity items, although you can opt not to show any Featured Listings)
- **Listings** (select the order in which you want items displayed in your store as well as the layout)
- **Category Type** (choose either Ebay OR your own store categories to display on the left navigation bar of your store)

Promotions: Under **Merchandising** on the left-hand column in the *Marketing* section of your *Seller Hub* is the **Promotions** link. Ebay has recently added a lot of new ways for us to promote our listings, including:

- **Order size discounts** incentivize buyers to spend more money in your store by setting minimum discounts, such as B1G1 FREE offers and percentage/dollar-off discounts on quantity and order total minimums.
- **Shipping discounts** that let buyers save on shipping when they buy more from you.
- **Codeless coupons** allow you to create URLs that you can share via social media and email that give your customers percentage or dollar-off discounts.
- **Volume pricing** incentivizes buyers to buy more quantities of your items by setting discounts on multi-quantity purchases such as "save 15% when you buy two or more items".

Markdown Sale: Back over on the left-hand side of the *Marketing* page is the **Markdown sale** link. I use the feature the most when trying to drive sales; Ebay used to call it **Markdown Manager**. By clicking on the **blue Create a promotion button** on the upper right-hand side of the page and choosing **Sale event + mark-**

down from the drop-down menu, you will be taken to the **Create a sale event** page.

Ebay offers you three different **Choose your discount** options:

- **Take a percent off each item** (the drop-down menu offers you the option of anywhere from 5% to 80% off)
- **Take a dollar amount off of each item** (the drop-down menu offers you the option of anywhere from $5 to $1500 off)
- **Free shipping for all discounted items** (in addition to the percentage or dollar amount discount)

Let's say you want to run a 30% off sale. You would enter "30" as the percentage off discount and then click on the **blue Select items button.** You will then be taken to a new screen to **Select Items individually** OR **Create rules using categories.** I have always used the *Select Items individually* option, but you can play around with both choices to see which you like best.

When I choose to *Select Items individually*, I am taken to a new screen to see all my active *Fixed Price* listings. I can select all my items or narrow them down by **category, price**, and/or **days on-site**. I can bulk select everything I have listed or manually check each item I want to be placed into the sale.

I typically run my sales on all the items in my store, so I usually auto-select all my listings. Note that you can only select up to 500 listings for each sale you create, so if you have a large store, the *Create rules using categories* option may work better for you. There is no better way than the other; it just depends on what works best for you.

Back to the sale example: You have chosen to *Select Items* individually. Let us say that you have 400 items listed; you can easily select all of them at once to be included in your sale. You then click on the **blue Confirm selections button**, which will take you to a screen showing all of the items selected for your sale. You have the option to **Remove** any listings you want OR to click on the **blue Add more items button** before clicking on the **blue Save and review button.**

After clicking the **Save and review** button, the final screen to set up your sale will appear, the **Review your sale event** page. Here you can enter a Sale event name, which only you will see. You could enter "30% off sale", for instance. You will be able to **review your Discount type and items** (in this case, 30% off 400 items; you have another chance here to edit these options).

Next is the **Date range**. You will need to select a start date and time AND an end date and time. I typically set my sale to start immediately and to end a week later. Finally, under the **Sale event banner**, you type in your **Sale event description** ("Save 30% Off Everything!" as an example) and **Select sale event image** (Ebay will give you three of your listing thumbnails to choose from, or you can upload a different one).

The last section of this page is the **Preview sale event tile**, which shows you what customers will see on their end. If everything looks good, you simply click on the **blue Launch button** at the bottom of the page to start your sale!

Note that you can pause, edit, or end your sale at any time. It can take Ebay an hour or two to get your sale up and running, so do not worry if you do not see your items marked down immediately after clicking on *Launch*. Once your sale is live, be sure to promote it via social media and on your website if you have one.

Promoted Listings: You can utilize the free social media platforms to drive customers to your Ebay Store. And Ebay allows you to run sales for free, too. However, you will want to consider one more piece of marketing, although it is not free; and that is *Promoted Listings.*

Promoted Listings are a relatively new offering from Ebay, and it is one that I use all day, every day. With so many other people selling on Ebay, I have found that I need to pay for *Promoted Listings* to remain competitive.

Ebay describes *Promoted Listings* as helping "your items stand out among billions of listings on Ebay and be seen by millions of active buyers when they're browsing and searching for what you are selling, helping to increase the likelihood of a sale. You only pay when an item sells. *Promoted Listings* is available only to Above Standard and Top-Rated Sellers with recent sales activity."

Ebay points to four key benefits of *Promoted Listings:*

1. **Boost Visibility:** Your items are more likely to sell when more people see them. *Promoted Listings* puts your items in front of more buyers, boosting visibility by up to 36%.
2. **Pay Only For Sale:** You are not charged until a buyer clicks on your promoted listing and purchases the promoted item within 30 days.
3. **Guided Set-Up:** Ebay's guidance tools help take the guesswork out and suggest which items to promote and at what cost.
4. **Detailed Reporting:** Access detailed campaign metrics and sales reports to monitor performance and fine-tune your campaigns.

From **Seller Hub**, click on **Marketing** and choose **Promoted Listings** from the drop-down menu. Here you will see the **Summary** date of any *Promoted Listings* you have already run, and you can set up a new campaign by clicking on the **blue Create new campaign button** near the bottom of the page.

After clicking on *Create new campaign,* a new screen will appear titled **How do you want to create your campaign?** You have two choices: **Select listings individually** OR **Select listings in bulk**. I always choose the *Select listings individually* option as, for me, it is easier than the bulk option.

By choosing to *Select listings individually,* a new screen comes up where I can select each eligible item to add to my *Promoted Listing.* When I run *Promoted Listing* campaigns, I include all the items in my store, making a simple bulk selection to choose all my listings. I then click on the **blue Set ad rate button** to continue to the **Set ad rates** screen.

Note that your ad rate is the percentage of the final sale price, excluding shipping and taxes, that you are willing to pay to have your listing promoted. You cannot set ad rates below 1% or above 100%. You are only charged a fee when your item sells within 30 days of the customer clicking on it.

Ebay will default to showing you their **Suggested ad rates**, which are typically relatively high. My trick is to click on the **blue Change your ad rate strategy button** and select **Apply single ad rate.** I then choose a rate of 1% or 2% for all my items. I have found this to be just as successful as choosing the Ebay suggested rates, but it saves me a lot of money as I am not paying the higher percentage.

After choosing my rate, I click on the **blue Review button** at the bottom of the page. The third and final screen is brought up, which is **Name your campaign**. I enter a name that only I will see (Ebay makes you write something in this field, but buyers will not see it). I then click on the **blue Launch button** at the bottom of the screen to start the *Promoted Listings* campaign.

After clicking on the Launch button, you will be taken back to the main **Promoted Listings** page you started at. At the bottom of this page, you will see your **Campaigns**, both active and ended. Ebay will default to running your campaigns continuously, but I like to have my campaigns run for shorter periods, anywhere from a week to a month. I have found them to be more successful when they have an end date, and I then start a brand-new campaign. And just as with running a sale, you can pause, edit, or end your *Promoted Listings* at any time.

A website, social media pages, branding, sales, and promoted listings. There are so many options available to you as an Ebay seller to market your listings. While it can all seem overwhelming, trust me that promotion efforts become second nature after a while. The increase in sales will make all your extra time and effort worth it in the end!

CHAPTER ELEVEN:

MANAGING AN EBAY STORE

To open an Ebay Store or not? That is the question I have been asked more times than I can count since I started giving out Ebay advice in my books and on my YouTube channel!

The general rule of thumb is that if you consistently have at least 100 items listed on Ebay, then an Ebay Store makes sense financially. Ebay Store owners get discounts on both listing and final value fees. Ebay currently offers five different store subscriptions:

Starter Store:

- For occasional sellers who want an entry-level option
- $4.95 a month when you commit to an annual subscription
- 250 free fixed-price listings per month
- 30-cent listing fee above allocation

Basic Store:

- For sellers who want lower selling fees
- $21.95 a month when you commit to an annual subscription

- 1,000 free fixed-price listings per month
- 250 free auction listings
- 25-cent listing fee above allocation
- $25 Ebay branded shipping supply coupon every quarter

Premium Store:

- For sellers wanting lower listing fees and more business tools
- $59.95 a month for an annual subscription
- 10,000 free fixed-price listings
- 500 free auction listings for collectibles and fashion
- 10-cent fixed-price listing fee above allocation
- 15-cent auction listing fee above allocation
- $50 Ebay branded shipping supply coupon every quarter

Anchor Store:

- For high-volume sellers who want dedicated support
- $299.95 a month
- 25,000 free fixed-price listings per month
- 1,000 free auction listings per month
- 5-cent fixed-price listing fee above allocation
- 10-cent auction listing fee above allocation
- $150 Ebay branded shipping supply coupon every quarter
- Access to dedicated customer support by phone or email

Enterprise:

- For the pros with large catalogs and high transaction volumes
- $2,999.95 a month
- 100,000 free fixed-price listings per month

- 2,500 free auction listings per month
- 5-cent fixed-price listing fee above allocation
- 10-cent auction listing fee above allocation
- $150 Ebay branded shipping supply coupon every quarter
- Access to dedicated customer support by phone or email
- Access to free sales-tax calculation assistance from Vertex

All Ebay Store subscribers receive:

- Access to Terapeak Research
- Access to Promoted Listings
- Access to Promotions Manager
- Customizable Storefront Homepage
- Customized Store Web Address
- Controllable "Featured Items"
- Store Categories

My favorite features of having an Ebay Store are:

A personalized URL (web address) that you can give customers to send them directly to your store. This shortened URL is easy to put on business cards or other enclosures. I include my URL store link on all my social media sites, in my books, and on YouTube to drive traffic directly to my store.

The ability to personalize your Ebay Store's look by changing the colors, adding your logo, and utilizing "Pages" to provide your customers with more information. To access these customization tools, go to your Ebay Store's front page and click on the **Manage My Store** button in the upper right-hand corner of the page. There are a lot of features here to explore under the **Store Management column** on the left-hand side of the page, including:

Advertising Preferences: Ebay allows you to control the information you share regarding how the site uses cookies, partners with advertisers, and collects information from your devices. You can edit these selections, i.e., turn them off or on at any time. Mine are always set to "No."

Permissions: Add authorized users, such as employees, to your Ebay account.

Store Categories: One of the best features of having an Ebay Store is creating specific item categories. Not only can buyers narrow down their search when they are looking at your store, but it is helpful for you as a seller to keep track of your inventory.

The great thing about categories is you can add and delete them as you see fit. Perhaps you have a large stock of camera equipment to sell, so you create a "Camera" category. However, after you have sold all the cameras, you can delete the "Camera" category or simply leave it in your store set up as only categories with active listings show up. Inactive categories will still be visible to you in the "Manage Your Store" section, but they will only be seen by customers if or when you add items to them.

I like to arrange my categories alphabetically. While you can break down categories into subcategories, you are usually fine merely listing in the main category unless you have thousands of items listed.

Make sure to spell and capitalize your categories appropriately. I like to put mine in all capitals, such as "COLLECTIBLES" and "COFFEE MUGS." I personally think typing a category like "BIBLES & HYMNALS" looks a lot better than "bibles and hymnals." However, if I add in sub-categories, I type them in sentence case, i.e., "Bibles and Hymnals."

Once you have an Ebay Store, you will be able to select the store categories for your items whenever you go to list something. You can list in two store categories. Note that the store categories are different from the Ebay categories, where you get one free and must pay for a second. With your store categories, both selections are free.

Edit Store: *Customize your Store Name, Billboard (banner), Log, Description, Featured Listings,* and *Display*

Subscriber Discounts: Here is where you can access your **quarterly Ebay Shipping Supply Coupon** (for *Starter, Premium, Anchor,* and *Enterprise* store levels). Every quarter, Ebay provides a shipping supply coupon that you can apply toward Ebay branded shipping supplies, including boxes, poly and bubble mailers, shipping tape, tissue paper, and stickers.

TIP: Always spend a little bit more than your shipping coupon amount. You can only use your coupon code once, so if you do not spend it all the first time, you will lose any overage. My favorite shipping supplies are the stickers!

Other discounts for store subscribers include Gusto Payroll, Bench Bookkeeping, Ebay Wholesale Deals, PayPal Shopping Offers, and Frooition Design Services.

Email Marketing: A rarely discussed feature of having an Ebay Store is that you can promote it by sending emails to anyone who adds you to their *Saved Sellers List.* You can also offer a *Store newsletter link* on your store's homepage. Ebay provides you with several user-friendly templates for you to customize when you want to update your subscribers about any sales, special promotions, or exciting new items in your store.

Listing Frame: Set up a custom listing frame that will appear in all your listings. It can include your store's listing header and a left-navigation bar with links to your store's categories. This is a fun section to play around with to give your listings a customized look.

Note that some links are repeated under the *Manage Your Store* page, such as *Permissions* and *Advertisement Preferences*. Also, *Manage Promotions* and *Markdown Manager* will take you back over to those sections of your *Seller Hub* that we discussed earlier in this chapter. The *Manage Your Store* page has gone through some changes in recent years, especially now that *Seller Hub*, not **My Ebay**, is the main page Ebay sellers use to manage their accounts.

Time Away: While only Ebay Store subscribers used to be able to put their stores and listings on vacation, now all Ebay users have access to what is now referred to as **Time Away**. Whether you need a break due to personal reasons or you are going on a vacation, anyone who sells on Ebay can now **Schedule Time Away.**

You can choose to allow sales to continue by editing your handling time, or you can pause your sales until you return. I always choose to pause sales as if I cannot have my store open; it is because I am too busy to attend to it properly. Therefore, I do not want to have to deal with customer questions. By pausing sales, your items are still visible on Ebay's site, but buyers cannot purchase them. *The Time Away* feature only applies to *Fixed Price* items, so make sure you have ended all *Auctions* before activating the *Time Away* feature.

If my Ebay sales are slow, I use the trick of turning my *Time Away* settings on overnight and then back off the next day. This seems to cause my listings to get "rebooted" in the Ebay system and show up as newly listed items. While there is no official word from Ebay that this is true, most sellers report that they see a spike in sales after using the *Time Away* feature. I have always gotten sales when I reactivated my listings the following day. I refer to this as "jiggling my store switch"!

To access your *Time Away* options, click on the **My Ebay** link at the top of your Ebay account page. Click on the **Account tab,** and you will find **Time Away** linked under **Selling** on the left-hand column of the page.

Store vs. No Store: One of the most common questions I get about selling on Ebay is whether or not to open an Ebay Store. As I mentioned earlier, the general rule of thumb is that if you are consistently going to have at least 100 items listed on Ebay, then a store makes the most financial sense. If you have not already subscribed to an Ebay Store, you can always start with the lowest level and upgrade later. If you sign up for a store under the yearly rate, not the month-to-month rate, note that if you cancel or downgrade your store before your year is up that you will have to pay the difference from the monthly and yearly rate.

Sellers often feel that they must get their Ebay Store "ready" before opening it to the public. However, you need to remember that an Ebay Store is not like a brick-and-mortar store. Most customers will access your listings in Ebay's search, not through your actual store. It will only be after you start promoting your store's URL address via social media that people will get to your storefront to see what you have for sale. Once you subscribe to an Ebay Store, your listings will automatically be placed there. **You cannot hide your store from users until you deem it "ready."**

While I encourage you to have a great store design, your priority should be getting your items listed. Once a listing is live, it will automatically be visible in your Ebay Store. If you find that your sales are going well and that your listings are increasing, you can always upgrade your store subscription level; in fact, Ebay will likely message you with special offers to upgrade your store if it is performing well.

Many sellers think having an Ebay Store is all about the customer's experience. But the truth is that sellers gain a lot more from a store in terms of reduced fees and organization than buyers do from shopping in a "store" setting. Because most customers will find your listings in Ebay's search, many will not click through your actual Ebay Store. But even though most buyers will not venture into your "store," it does not mean you should not have one, as the savings on listing fees alone is typically worth the price of your subscription!

CHAPTER TWELVE:

TAKING EBAY TO THE NEXT LEVEL

When you own your own business, there is no difference between part-time versus full-time in terms of the hours you will work. Selling on Ebay on even a part-time basis can be an all-day, everyday commitment; you need to be available to answer customer questions and to ship out orders promptly. If I will be away from my home for more than 24 hours, I put my Ebay Store on vacation, now called Time Away.

But when I talk about a part-time versus full-time Ebay business, I am really talking about income. I view a full-time Ebay business as one that provides the same income level as an average 40-hour-a-week job, enough to completely support one person by covering all their living expenses. For some, however, a full-time income means making enough money to support an entire family.

Only you know the level of income you want and need, determining how many hours you put into Ebay. The great thing about Ebay is that if you want more money, you just need to put more time into putting up new listings. Consistently listing new items to Ebay is the fundamental key to making money on the site.

The vast majority of Ebay sellers who view reselling as their business are part-time. Many rely on a spouse's income for most of the household budget. They themselves may also work another part-time or even a full-time job in addition to Ebay to earn enough money to support their family. Benefits such as health insurance are also a big reason many Ebay sellers have other income sources.

While reselling on Ebay can be very profitable, it can be hard to cover all household expenses and insurance costs by only selling online, especially as sales can go up and down depending on the time of year. I sell a lot from October through March, but June and July are painfully slow.

However, do not let that discourage you from your dream of starting a full-time home-based Ebay business! With a ton of hard work and dedication, you can make a full-time living on Ebay. However, I believe it is best to start slowly by viewing an Ebay business first to earn a little extra money, then expanding it to an actual part-time job. If you want to pursue it full-time after that, then go for it. If you follow the business advice in this chapter, you will already be prepared as your Ebay business grows.

Perhaps you are a stay-at-home mom or dad looking to supplement your spouse's full-time income. Ebay can be an excellent job for you as it offers the flexibility of staying home with your children while running your own business. Plus, you retain the benefits from your spouse's job.

If you already have a job, I would advise keeping it and growing your Ebay business slowly. I would never tell someone with a good-paying job and benefits to quit it to sell on Ebay. However, maybe you have found yourself without steady employment due to the tough job market. If you need a job now and see self-employment as your only option, there is no better home-based business, in my opinion, than Ebay.

Whether you go part-time or full-time, earn a few thousand dollars a year, or an income in the six figures, make sure you treat Ebay as a business. Even if you do not, Uncle Sam certainly will as, if you sell more than $600 on the site in a year, Ebay will issue you a 1099 tax form.

Speaking of taxes…oh, how they make people nervous. I get asked a lot about whether people should get a **Sales Tax Permit** and/or an **Employer Identification Number** for their Ebay business. The answer is…. well, it depends.

Sales Tax Permit: If you plan to purchase items from wholesale companies, you will need a Sales Tax Permit. A *Sales Tax Permit* allows you to buy products at wholesale cost and not pay taxes on them. However, having a *Sales Tax Permit* means that you will need to collect and remit taxes on anything you sell to customers within your state.

Fortunately, Ebay now handles the collection and remittance of sales tax on the sellers' behalf. When a customer buys an item from you, if they live in a state that requires sales tax to be charged, the customer will pay the sales tax, but Ebay will then automatically route that tax to the respective state.

However, if you have a *Sales Tax Permit*, you will still have to file sales tax quarterly with your state. So, if you do not plan to use a *Sales Tax Permit* to purchase items at wholesale, you are better off not getting one so that you do not have to worry about taxes.

Note that most liquidation companies do not require a *Sales Tax Permit* for you to buy from them. While wholesale companies act as a middleman between the manufacturer and retailer and usually require retailers to provide a *Sales Tax Permit*, liquidation companies buy from the retailers themselves, looking to offload returns, damages, and overstocks. So, if you plan to buy liquidation to resell, chances are you will not need a *Sales Tax Permit*.

Employer Identification Number (EIN): An *Employer Identification Number* or *EIN* is for people who plan to hire employees. However, some wholesale companies do require an *EIN* to place an order from them. An *EIN* is free and easy to apply for. Just as most liquidation companies do not require resellers to have a Sales Tax Permit, most do not require an *EIN*, either.

Both *Sales Tax Permits* and *EINs* place a tax reporting burden on you that is avoidable if you do not have them or do not use them. Sometimes I can get a discount on liquidation by using my *Sales Tax Permit*, but I rarely take advantage of it as it is one more tax loophole to deal with at tax time.

Business Insurance: If you plan to have an ample supply of inventory, you will want to carry business insurance to protect it in case of fire, theft, or other damage. You may also be liable for anyone who is injured coming to your home or business, including delivery people. If you plan to store thousands of dollars' worth of merchandise in your home, you want to consider insuring it all.

If you plan to sell on Ebay for other people via consignment, you will need to get insurance to cover any damage to or loss of their items. You also want to protect yourself from consignment clients coming to your home and being injured. Call around to various insurance agencies and ask if they offer home-based business insurance coverage. If they do, ask for a free quote.

Health Insurance: If you have a spouse whose health insurance plan you can join, you are luckier than me. I have been purchasing my own health insurance since 2005, and I have paid upwards of $600 per month for my premiums, co-pays, and prescription drugs.

The **Affordable Care Act** now makes health insurance coverage more accessible and affordable for millions of Americans with the available tax credits. However, eligibility to buy insurance off the exchange is dependent on several factors, so make sure you find out if you qualify for ACA insurance before you quit your job to sell on Ebay. Visit healthcare.gov for more information.

If you are looking to Ebay to be your full-time income, you must examine the insurance costs involved as you will likely spend more on insurance than office supplies. And it is not just health insurance but also life insurance, injury insurance, sick time, vacation time, and retirement accounts. Again, you do not want to give up a good-paying job and benefits for an Ebay career unless you are 100% sure it will provide for you and your family!

If you are serious about making Ebay an actual business, it is helpful to talk to someone with business experience. If you want to work from home selling on Ebay for a part-time or full-time income, two organizations can assist you: **SCORE** and the **Small Business Administration**.

SCORE stands for the Service Corp of Retired Executives. SCORE volunteers are former business owners who offer FREE, confidential counseling to anyone starting or expanding a business. They have 350 chapters in the United States, so you will likely be able to find an office near you.

Note that SCORE volunteers are retired and older; while they do have a lot of business experience, they may not know about Ebay or online retailing. However, they can help you figure out any local or state laws regarding home-based businesses; and they will know some necessary information regarding taxes and permits. SCORE volunteers can also help you craft a business plan.

To learn more about SCORE and to find an office near you, visit Score.org.

The **Small Business Administration,** or **SBA**, offers confidential counseling and classes to anyone wanting to start a business, as well as services for those already running a company. SBA employees can provide you with information on what you need to operate a business in your area, including permits, licenses, and taxes.

Most offices have a small library of business books you can borrow, as well as computer labs. Classes are incredibly low-cost. They also offer incubator spaces for businesses needing a start-up location. As with SCORE, SBA staff can assist you in writing up a business plan, which at the very least, is a guide to helping you along with your business, and at most, is crucial if you want to get funding.

To learn more about the SBA and to find an office near you, visit SBA.gov.

Ebay's Seller Help: Ebay itself is a fantastic resource for both new and experienced sellers. Check out the *Seller Help* link at the top of your *Seller Hub* page for articles, tutorials, and videos. When I started my Ebay business, I studied every single section on their site; and it helped me with everything from listing to shipping.

The Ebay Community: When I first started selling on Ebay, *The Ebay Community* (previously referred to as the "message boards") was a wealth of information for me. You will find the link to *Community* at the very bottom of all Ebay pages.

There are several sections of *The Ebay Community*, including:

- **Seller News:** Announcements and Seller Town Halls
- **Knowledge Base:** Buying & Selling Q&A, Commonly Asked Questions, and Community Mentor Corner
- **Discussions:** New To Ebay, Buying & Selling, Inside Ebay, Categories, and Seller Updates
- **Groups:** Ebay Categories, Business Insights, Regional

Groups, Special Interest Groups, Payments, Ebay Upfront, Meetup Organizers
- **Ebay Podcast:** The Ebay for Business Podcast

Facebook: If you have a Facebook account, you will find many groups dedicated to selling on Ebay. The **Ebay for Business Facebook** page also posts daily; it is the best place to go to get up-to-the-minute announcements directly from the company. And you can join the private **Ebay for Business Podcast Group**, too.

Instagram: There is an active "reselling community" on Instagram that shares tips and tricks for selling on all the online platforms, including Ebay. If you are new to Instagram, you can follow my account (which is linked on the last page of this book) and find other resellers through me. Whether you need specific questions answered or just want to find fellow resellers to connect with, you will find a great community on Instagram!

YouTube Videos: Ebay has its own YouTube channel where they post videos of seminars from Ebay events. There are also a ton of reselling videos made by Ebay sellers, including myself. So many Ebay sellers are sharing their tips and tricks for making money on their own YouTube channels. Whether you are looking for tutorials, hauls, or thrift-with-me videos, you will find them all within the reselling community on YouTube!

CHAPTER THIRTEEN:

EBAY ACCOUNTING MADE EASY

I get so many questions from Ebay sellers who, like me, are not very confident with their math skills. However, while it is important to keep adequate accounting records for your Ebay business, it really is not hard at all once you establish a basic system for your recordkeeping. In this chapter, I will explain exactly how to make the Ebay accounting process as easy for you as it is for me. Trust me, if I can keep my Ebay records using this system, so can you!

Should you hire an accountant?

Before we get to the actual accounting system, we need to cover some other important issues surrounding the finances of selling on Ebay, including hiring an accountant. Please note that these are my experiences; as with anything, be sure to do your own research on all aspects of your business, especially when it comes to accounting and taxes, as laws vary by state. When having doubts, it is always best to consult with a tax professional in your area.

When I started my business in 2005, I met with an accountant who set up the bookkeeping system I will be sharing with you in this chapter. The simple system he set up for me years ago still works for me today. It has stayed the same whether I was selling gift baskets locally, wholesale items on Ebay and Amazon, or secondhand items on Ebay, Etsy, and Poshmark. I knew my accountant well from my previous office job and have always trusted his advice and knowledge.

However, while I keep my own books throughout the year, I hire my accountant to file my taxes. Tackling my own tax returns is not something I personally feel comfortable with. Because I have an easy system for my bookkeeping, I simply keep track of everything throughout the year and then turn it all over to my accountant at tax time. Since I have kept good records for the year, he can quickly and easily file my taxes for me, which drastically cuts down on the bill he sends me for his tax filing services.

It is essential to understand the difference between keeping your own accounting books and then hiring someone to file taxes versus hiring someone to do all your accounting. I keep my own books, but my accountant files my taxes. If my accountant kept my books for me and filed my taxes on top of it, I would be paying him a hefty monthly fee. I do know some small business owners who meet with their accountants quarterly to manage their books. It really depends on the person and the business itself as to how often someone should meet with their accountant over the course of a year.

If you are comfortable filing your own taxes, you will still be able to use the accounting system I show you later in this book. However, if you want to hire someone to do them for you, you will save a lot of time and money by having your accounting system in place. That way, when tax time comes around, you can simply hand over your records to a tax professional, and they will be able to file them for you quickly.

Again, the less time an accountant or tax preparer must spend sorting out your records, the cheaper their bill will be. While it may be tempting just to save up all your receipts and give them to someone a few days before April 15th, it is so much easier and cheaper to keep your own records and simply have someone file your returns for you.

There is no need for me to give my accountant a stack of receipts at tax time or for me to go over all my credits and debits line by line as the system I use summarizes my gross sales and net expenses in one basic sheet of paper. I simply give my accountant my gross sales totals and my expense totals using the easy accounting system I have in place, and he handles the rest. At this point, I could probably just follow my accountant's template and file my own returns; but I prefer the security of having a CPA prepare and file my taxes for me.

Whether or not to hire an accountant is a personal choice. I must admit that I feel safer hiring someone to file my taxes for me. The IRS loves to audit small businesses, and I feel that having an accountant handling my returns offers an extra layer of protection for me. I even sign a form that gives my accountant permission to talk to the IRS on my behalf if any questions arise.

Another bonus of hiring an accountant to file your returns is that they are specifically trained to get you the most deductions possible. Most Ebay businesses are run out of homes (mine is!), so there are many additional deductions available that are not for people who run brick-and-mortar stores. I can deduct the space I use in my home for my business, including property taxes and utilities. I also get deductions for using my car for business. My accountant keeps all this information in my file and just fills it in on my tax forms every year.

One final benefit for me of having an accountant has been that he can set me up to pay my income taxes every quarter rather than all at once at the end of the year. Using the previous year's returns, he estimates what I may have to pay the following year. He then prepares tax forms for me to submit every three months. I simply cut a check and mail in the forms, both to my state as well as to the Federal government. Sometimes I still owe a bit more money in taxes at the end of the year, but that just means that I made more money. And with the changing tax laws, occasionally, I end up with a refund.

While it is nice to hope that you will always get a tax refund every year, paying quarterly definitely protects you during the years when you may have underpaid and then owe money. Paying my income tax quarterly prevents me from getting hit with a potentially massive tax bill from the IRS at the end of the year. If, at the end of the year, it turns out I have overpaid on my quarterly tax returns, I will get a refund. And since I am not skilled in IRS laws, I need my accountant to do this for me. When it comes to taxes, I would rather overpay than underpay as the IRS will eventually come to collect what they are owed.

If you do feel you need to hire an accountant or tax professional to prepare your taxes, be sure to ask around to your friends and family for their recommendations. There are many big accounting firms around that will charge you an arm and a leg to handle your returns. But many people run small offices or even work part-time from home who can do your taxes for a lot less.

Get recommendations from your friends and family, and then make a few calls. Ask what they charge for tax filing, and ask if they do free initial consultations. Also, be sure to ask if they have experience filing taxes for home-based e-commerce businesses, specifically Ebay, as they come with their own set of rules. If you use the accounting techniques that I will be sharing with you in this chapter, you will be able to tell potential CPAs that you keep your own books and are just looking for someone to submit your tax filings every year.

However, if the accountants you interview offer a free or low-cost initial consultation, take advantage of it. If you have started keeping your own records, take them with you to the meeting to see if they can work based on what you have or if they want to make changes to your system. Having a good accountant on your side is never wrong when running a business; plus, you can write their fee off as a business expense!

If you feel confident filing your own taxes, you can skip hiring an accountant. However, note that it is good to educate yourself on your state's specific tax laws. A little research can save you a lot of grief at tax time. Fortunately, you can use two FREE resources: **SCORE** and the **Small Business Administration**, both of which I discussed earlier in this book. Most large cities have these services available; a quick Google search will bring up the offices closest to you.

Both SCORE and the SBA can advise you about the potential need for you to hire an accountant, and they can also help you determine whether you want to set up your Ebay business as a **sole proprietorship** or an **LLC**. The vast majority of Ebay business owners are sole proprietors, someone who owns an unincorporated business by themselves. An LLC is a business that has legally been set up as an organization. Different tax laws apply to each. There are more tax benefits with an LLC, but an LLC is much more complicated to set up and complex to maintain. If you are going to form an LLC, you will definitely have to hire a CPA to assist you.

Again, a SCORE volunteer, SBA employee, or an accountant can talk to you about whether a sole proprietorship or LLC is best for you. Still, unless you plan to hire employees, you will likely be operating as a sole proprietor. That means that you will be filing your business taxes under your given legal name.

As a sole proprietor myself, my legal name is technically my business name as far as the IRS is concerned. However, my name is followed by D.B.A., which means "Doing Business As" on bank statements and permits.

Note that a D.B.A. can also affect how you cash checks; most banks will only cash checks to accounts that match the checks' name, including the D.B.A. So, if you get checks made out to your D.B.A. name, a bank likely will not deposit them into an account that only has your name on it. This is something you will want to check with your bank about. If they feel you should have an account under your D.B.A., it should be easy to set up and may even link to your personal account.

Some banks may also require that you file a business license in your city with the D.B.A. name. If they do, do not panic, as the process is simple and relatively inexpensive to complete at your local courthouse. Again, your bank will be able to best advise you on this.

If you plan just to flip finds from garage sales, though, I would not worry about having a D.B.A. You can certainly create a business name for the fun of it, but legally just your name will likely suffice. However, suppose you plan to grow your business beyond just a part-time gig. In that case, you will want to consult a lawyer or your accountant to learn about the benefits of changing your business structure to an LLC. Even though my business has changed and grown over the years, neither my accountant nor I have felt it necessary to convert my business to an LLC.

Opening a Business Bank Account: The whole point of selling on Ebay is to MAKE MONEY! Therefore, it is a good idea to get a separate checking account dedicated solely to your business. Having a business account separate from your personal account makes keeping track of business income and expenses so much easier.

As I discussed earlier, most banks will not cash checks that are made out to your business name into your personal account. So, if you plan to be receiving any payments using your D.B.A. name, a business account might be necessary.

If you are not already a credit union member, look for one in your area as they usually offer free account setup, free checking, and no ATM fees. You will want to get checks under your business account so that you can buy things such as office supplies directly from your business account. I write very few checks, but I sometimes use them at estate sales when purchasing inventory.

Having a dedicated credit card for your business is also a good idea. I have a credit card that I keep on file with Ebay as a backup funding source and use it when I buy something on the site.

In the rare instance that I must take a package to the Post Office for shipping (I do most of my shipping from home with the postage deducted directly from my Ebay balance), I use the credit card to pay for the postage. I buy shipping supplies locally from Staples and Sam's Club and online from several different companies; all supplies are charged to my cards. I also use credit cards when buying inventory at thrift stores, and a few of the estate sale companies in my area also accept them.

Charging business supplies, services, and inventory onto one credit card makes it easy for me to track my expenses. I chose a business credit card that offered rewards, too, so that I get something back for using it. However, be careful to pay off your credit card balance every month, or you will soon be using all your profits to pay for credit card fees. When I sold new gift items that I bought at wholesale, I had to order them using a credit card; and the fees added up quickly.

Using one card is ideal as I can pull up the monthly statements online while doing my monthly bookkeeping. I can easily see what I spent, where I spent it, and what I spent it on, making it quick and easy to itemize my expenses.

My Easy Accounting System: Ah, here we are at the heart of this chapter: How to keep your Ebay accounting records. This system is so straightforward; trust me, anyone can do it if I can do it. To say that math is not my strong suit is an understatement! But even I can do my Ebay books this way.

How much money can you make selling on Ebay? As much as you are willing to work for! Many people sell on Ebay just for some extra money. Some do it as a part-time job. And others have expanded it into their full-time income. However, bringing in any amount of money requires accounting. As much as you may want to avoid bookkeeping, trust me when I say that when tax time rolls around, you will be so glad you started and stuck with a system at the beginning of the year. You cannot hide from Uncle Sam; the IRS will eventually catch up with you. And this accounting system is just too easy not to do!

When I started my business, I paid my accountant $300 for an hour-long meeting for him to set up my bookkeeping system. And it is this same easy system that I am about to lay out for you. Basically, it is just a check register, like the one you probably have in your checkbook. I keep track of my debits and credits and then hand off the totals to my accountant at the end of the year.

You can use a computer spreadsheet, a paper bookkeeping book, or just a plain notebook. Or you can use my **2022 Ebay Seller Planner & Accounting Ledger**, available on Amazon, which has this system all laid out.

Your business accounting breaks down into two categories: **DEBITS** and **CREDITS.**

Debits are your expenses (withdraws) on the check register.

Credits are the funds you earn (deposits) on the check register.

Just like you use your check register to log your checks written and deposited, you will track your Ebay income and expenses the same way.

Check # (the number on your check)

Date (the date of the transaction)

Transaction (the transaction itself, such as "USPS" or "PayPal")

Debit (the amount of money spent)

Credit (the amount of money deposited into your business account)

Balance (the total running balance after the most recent debit or credit)

And that is all you need to track your day-to-day running numbers. Yes, it really is that simple!

At the end of the month, you will break your numbers down further to itemize your expenses. Here is how I break down my numbers (I will use September as an example):

SEPTEMBER CREDITS:

Ebay Gross Sales: This number can easily be found by going to your **Seller Hub**, clicking on the **Performance** tab at the top of the page, and choosing **Sales** from the drop-down menu.

Other Gross Sales: If you sell on other platforms, such as Poshmark or Etsy, or if you sell locally via Facebook Marketplace or at an antique mall booth, you can break out those sales numbers here; since this is an Ebay focused book, we will just stick to Ebay numbers for this example.

SEPTEMBER DEBITS/EXPENSES:

Ebay Fees: You can find a breakdown of your monthly Ebay fees under the **Performance** tab in **Seller Hub**; simply select

Summary from the drop-down menu to access this data. Even though Ebay automatically deducts your fees from your balance, you still need these numbers to account against your gross sales.

Simply pull up your Ebay seller account and your monthly invoice to find how much you owed in fees for each month. Note that this amount includes store subscriptions, listing fees, final value fees, and any other fees, such as those for *Promoted Listings*. You do not need to break down each of these fees for your records; you just need the grand total of all your fees for tax purposes.

PayPal Fees: If you have run any sales through PayPal, you can locate this number by logging into your PayPal account and selecting your monthly statement. Simply click on "Reports" at the top of the page, then click on "Statements" and select "Monthly." You can then generate a report of all your PayPal activity by month; the PayPal fees you paid are located under the "Fees" section.

Cost of Goods: How much you spent during the month on items to resell

Postage: The amount you spent on postage, whether paid by you or the customer, is also found in the **Summary** section under the **Performance** tab in your **Seller Hub**. Because your shipping costs were included in your gross sales number, it does not matter whether you or the buyer paid for shipping; you just include the **Shipping labels** amount for the month on this line.

Advertising: I include thank you cards in my packages, and occasionally I run Facebook and Instagram ads to promote my Ebay Store. Typically Promoted Listings would fall under Advertising, but I lump the Promoted Listing Fees under the general Ebay Fee category.

Office/Shipping Supplies: The total amount I spend on everything from labels and printer ink to poly mailers and bubble wrap is added here.

Website/Internet Services: I add together my monthly internet fee and how much I pay for my phone.

Sales Tax: Since Ebay now collects sales tax from customers and remits it to each state themselves, I will be dropping this category starting next year.

State Income Tax: I pay quarterly state income tax.

Federal Income Tax: I pay quarterly federal income tax.

Business Insurance: I carry insurance on my inventory.

Bank/Credit Card Fees: Any fees you pay for your business bank account. If you are using a business card for purchases, you will want to keep track of the fees you pay on the card, too.

Travel: Any travel costs (gas, hotel) associated with your reselling business, such as trips out of town to source or if you attend any Ebay events.

Meals: Any food purchased in conjunction with running your reselling business (business meals, not the food you eat during your workday).

Monthly Health Insurance Premiums: If you pay out of pocket for health insurance, include that amount here.

Prescription Drug Copays: Tally up your monthly prescription drug copays here.

Doctor Copays/Deductibles/Dentist: Keep track of any out-of-pocket expenses you pay for health care, including at the dentist.

Mileage: I use the app MileIQ to track my business mileage.

I can also claim a portion of my home as office space; my accountant has that figure already stored in my files and inputs it into my returns every year.

Now, let's look at how I keep track of my transactions during the course of the month, using a purchase of office supplies as an example:

Imagine that I purchase copy paper for $10 at Staples on February the 11th. On a checkbook-style ledger, I write "2/11" under "Date" and "Staples" under "Transaction." Since I spent money, I write "$10" under the "Debit" column. I then subtract $10 from the current "Balance" to give me my new business account balance.

See how this is done just as I would have if had I been using my household checkbook?

At the end of the month, I look through my "Debit" column. I add together all the expenses related to "Office/Shipping Supplies" and enter that number onto my monthly expenses sheet.

At the end of the year, I add up all the amounts under "Office/Shipping Supplies" to get my total yearly expenses for that section. That final number, which goes onto my year-end sheet, is the only number I have to provide my accountant with.

I do the same for the other expense categories, too, and I give all the category totals to my accountant at the end of the year.

There are a couple of shortcuts I use to track my expenses. First, I keep all business charges on one credit card; that way, I only have to look through one monthly statement to see where I spent money on office supplies and at estate sales or thrift stores.

Second, Ebay provides many useful statistics that make tracking your sales, fees, and postage costs a breeze via *Seller Hub*. I used to manually add up every individual shipping charge, but now that number is provided to me in one line in the *Summary* section of my *Performance* page.

All these numbers are essential to help you see how much money you are making by selling on Ebay. Figuring out your **NET** versus **GROSS** income is KEY to running any business.

GROSS income is the total amount of money, the "credits," you bring in BEFORE expenses are taken out.

NET income is the total amount of money you have left AFTER your expenses, the "debits," are taken out.

After you have accounted for all your expenses, or "debits," you will have your NET income, which is the actual PROFIT you made. **GROSS SALES minus EXPENSES equals NET PROFIT!**

At the end of the year, I total my monthly debits and credits and combine them into yearly totals. I give my accountant my GROSS sales number, which is the total of all my credits. I then give him all my EXPENSES, which are all my debits. Subtracting my DEBITS from the CREDITS gives me my NET income for the year, and the NET income is what I pay taxes on.

Since I have other sources of income (books, YouTube, affiliate marketing), I usually have several tax forms for my accountant to process. However, if your only business is Ebay, then you will either have the 1099 tax form Ebay provides you (if you sell over $600) or the numbers you have kept yourself for your accountant to work on (or for you to process if you are planning on filing taxes yourself).

As I noted on my accounting sheet, I also have other deductions that I give to my accountant, such as self-employed health insurance and prescription drug costs. I can also claim the areas of my house that I use for my business, including the utilities and property taxes.

Another thing I claim is the mileage from driving to the Post Office and going to estate sales and thrift stores. An easy way to do this is to keep a small notebook in your vehicle and write down your miles anytime you drive around on business. Or, as I said, you can use an app such as MileIQ.

My accountant has set up an income tax payment system for me, where I pay quarterly. He prepares four forms for me every year so that every quarter I mail a form and a check into the IRS. That way, I keep up on my income tax throughout the year and do not get hit with a hefty bill when I file my taxes. This is something he does as part of my yearly tax filing.

So, to recap: **My accounting system is basically a check register where I log my debits and credits.** I tally up the totals in each column at the end of the year and hand them off to my accountant, who then files my taxes.

There is no big box of receipts to keep track of. I do not have to spend hours in my accountant's office going through my records. It takes me about 30 minutes a month and around an hour at the end of the year to add up all my columns, and I then just give those numbers to my accountant. He factors in my deductions and files my tax returns for me.

EASY!!!

And to make it even easier for you, as I mentioned earlier, I also have reselling planners and accounting ledgers that I sell on Amazon. You can currently order my **2022 Ebay Seller Planner & Accounting Ledger,** which is an 8.5x11-inch book to help you keep track of your monthly and yearly sales and expenses. I also have versions for just **Poshmark** and **Etsy** and an all-in-one **Reseller** version for those who sell on multiple platforms.

Paying Yourself: Two questions I get asked a lot are, **"How much should I pay myself?"** and **"How much money should I reinvest in my business?"** After all your expenses are accounted for, and you know your net income, you will need to decide how much to keep for yourself and how much to put back into your business.

However, with Ebay, your sales, and therefore, your cash flow, can vary wildly, which makes answering these two questions nearly impossible. All I can really do in this instance is to share with you how I handle this division of paying myself versus re-investing in my business.

After filling out my accounting ledger at the end of the month, I see what my NET income for the month is. I pay all my personal bills (not my business expenses, as those were deducted for me to get my net income) from that total, and I am then left with a new amount.

If it has been an excellent month of sales, I will have extra money to take out for myself while setting aside some for buying more items to resell. However, if sales have been slow, I may find that there is not much money left. So, I must make a choice: put that money back in my business for supplies and inventory, or put it into my pocket for fun.

Let's say your NET income for January was $3000. Remember, NET means all your business expenses, including fees and inventory, have already been deducted. Out of that $3,000, you have $2,000 in personal bills that you need to pay, which leaves you with $1,000. After looking at prior months, you realize that you have spent around $500 a month to buy items to resell, so you decide to dedicate $500 to buy items in February, which leaves you with the remaining $500 for yourself.

Again, this is just an example. You always want to remember that you are selling on Ebay to make money for yourself, not to continually funnel into your business. Keeping a ledger will help you track your cash flow and expenses to make an informed decision about how much money to take out for you and how much to leave in for your business. Do not get caught in the trap of reinvesting everything you make back into Ebay; be sure to pay yourself.

In business, you must spend money to make money; selling on Ebay means you will be spending money on inventory and fees and supplies and taxes. In fact, during months where you are investing a lot into your business, you may find that you barely break even...or worse, even lose money. With that, here is some advice on how to save money when you are selling on Ebay.

1. Do not pay up for listing extras such as subtitles and second categories. Most of the "upgrades" Ebay offers are not worth the money.
2. Repurpose shipping supplies when you can and ask friends, family, neighbors, and co-workers to give you their extra boxes and packing peanuts.
3. When you do purchase shipping supplies, buy them in bulk to save money.
4. Plan your car trips to cut down on excessive gas usage.
5. Pay with cash as much as possible. If you do use a credit card, use only one. And try to pay off the balance every month to avoid interest charges.
6. Do not invest in fancy backdrops and expensive camera equipment. I use a white poster board from the dollar store for photos and use my iPhone to take my pictures.
7. Do not go sourcing until what you already have is listed. Shopping for inventory is the best part about reselling, but they cannot sell if your items are not listed. Your death pile is a money pile; do not bring any more items into your space until

you list what you have.
8. Always look at the available shipping options for each order before purchasing postage to see if you can save a bit of money by choosing a different service or carrier.
9. Utilize USPS FREE Carrier Pickup to pick up your Ebay packages to save a trip to the Post Office.
10. Do not invest in a fancy printer until you can pay for it in cash; I have run my business since 2005 without a DYMO, and you can, too

CHAPTER FOURTEEN:

CUSTOMER SERVICE

There is a lot of misinformation and even fear about buying and selling on Ebay. Rumors about scams and people getting ripped off are rampant. However, Ebay is overall a safe and secure place for both shoppers and sellers. In this chapter, I will hopefully clear up some common misconceptions about Ebay along with giving you some practical advice about protecting yourself as a seller on the site.

Ebay Support: Ebay support is available by phone or through messaging, although they do not make it easy to get in touch with a service representative. First, you will need to go to your **Seller Hub** and click on the **Seller Help** link in the page's upper right-hand corner. Here you can contact Ebay regarding the following issues:

- Request to remove improper feedback
- Request to remove defects that you believe to be out of your control
- Request a selling limit increase, which they will often grant if you have been meeting your seller performance standards
- Report an issue with a buyer who is not following Ebay's policies

If none of the above options apply to your situation, you can click on the **Need more help?** link at the bottom of the page. This will take you to Ebay's **Customer Service Selling** page with links to articles explaining all Ebay's policies. However, if you scroll all the way to the bottom of the page, there is another **Need more help?** section with a link for **Contact us.**

Once again, you will be brought to a page with various articles related to the problem you have identified. And again, at the bottom of this page is the third **Need more help?** area, although now you can choose to **Chat with our automated system** OR **Have us call you**. The call option will show you the wait time you can expect to receive a call.

Privacy/Safety: While the internet offers a level of anonymity, when you are on Ebay, there are some extra precautions you want to take. First and foremost is guarding your Ebay account information. Change your passwords often, and make them a combination of letters, numbers, and characters so that they will be nearly impossible to hack. The same goes for your PayPal account if you still are not enrolled in *Managed Payments.*

The only legitimate messages from Ebay will come to you via the Ebay messaging system that you access when you are logged into your account. At the top of your **Seller Hub** page is a link for **Messages**. Unless you have opted for copies of all messages that Ebay sends to you also be emailed to you, then the official messages from Ebay will only be found here.

Ebay does not send sellers direct email messages off the site; so, if you get an email from Ebay that is not also found in your *Messages* box, know that it is a scam. Scammers have been known to send emails to sellers disguised as messages from Ebay saying that you need to click a link within the email to reset your password or to login into your account. NEVER click on these email links, and do not give your Ebay or PayPal information to anyone claiming to be from the companies either by phone or email.

Keeping your home address private is another concern for Ebay sellers. I never worried too much about this until recently, when I finally got a P.O. Box so that I could make that my return mailing address for packages. Remember that your address will print out with your shipping label, so if you send out a lot of packages, you may want to make that address someplace other than home (such as your spouse's work or a P.O. Box). While this should not be a huge concern (after all, people have been using their home addresses for years), it may be something you want to consider.

I have a designated email set up expressly for Ebay, which all Ebay and PayPal communications go to. Although some large sellers, typically those with warehouses or brick-and-mortar stores, set up a number specifically for Ebay customers to call, I guard my phone number.

I also do not engage with customers outside of the Ebay system. Several times over the years, buyers have gotten a hold of my phone number and called my house, leaving me messages asking me to return their calls. I do not return calls from anyone who calls my home, nor should you. I do the same with direct emails; I delete them without responding. If an Ebay customer wants to communicate with me, they need to contact me directly through Ebay's *Messages* system.

Ebay Selling Practices Policy: It is important to remember that you need to adhere to Ebay's rules to utilize their site. As I have said before, Ebay is not YOUR business; it is a TOOL you use for your business. Ebay has given us the following policies, which all sellers are expected to follow:

- Promptly resolve customer issues
- Ship items on time, within your specified handling time

- Manage inventory and keep items well stocked
- Charge reasonable shipping and handling costs
- Specify shipping costs and handling time in the listing
- Follow through on your return policy
- Respond to buyers' questions promptly
- Be helpful, friendly, and professional throughout a transaction.
- Make sure the item is delivered to the buyer as described in the listing

Ebay warns sellers that not meeting buyers' expectations can result in the following issues for sellers:

- Not meeting the late shipment rate requirements
- Exceeding minimum requirements for the defect rate
- A bad experience for you and the buyer
- Low detailed seller ratings
- Negative or neutral feedback from a buyer
- A buyer requesting a return or reporting that an item was not received
- A buyer asking us to step in and help with a transaction issue

And issues with buyers affect your **Ebay's Transaction Defect Rate Requirements,** which is the percentage of transactions that have one or both of the following defects:

- eBay Money Back Guarantee and PayPal Purchase Protection cases closed without seller resolution
- Seller-initiated transaction cancellation

To meet Ebay's minimum standard selling requirements, sellers can only have up to 2% of transactions with one or more defects over the most recent evaluation period. To qualify as a **Top-Rated Seller**, which not only places your listings higher in search but also gives you fee discounts, you can only have up to 0.5% of transactions with one or more defects over the most recent evaluation period. Note that only your transactions with US buyers count toward your seller performance rating.

According to Ebay, "The defect rate won't affect your seller performance status until you have transactions with defects with at least five different buyers, or at least four different buyers to impact Top-Rated status within your evaluation period. You can have a maximum of 0.3% of eBay Money Back Guarantee, or PayPal Purchase Protection closed cases without seller resolution over the most recent evaluation period. That means the buyer reported they didn't receive an item, asked to return an item, or opened a PayPal Purchase Protection case; you weren't able to resolve it, the buyer asked us to step in and help, and we found you responsible."

"Sellers with 400 or more transactions over the past three months are evaluated based on the past three months, and sellers with fewer than 400 transactions are evaluated based on the past twelve months. Buyers won't see your defect rate. Keep in mind that buyers still see your feedback rating and all four detailed seller ratings."

In regards to shipping defects, Ebay states that sellers will "be recognized for on-time shipping if tracking shows your item was either shipped within the stated handling time or delivered by the estimated delivery date. If there's no tracking available, we'll check with your buyer. If your buyer confirms the item was delivered on time—you'll be recognized for on-time shipping."

Ebay will only consider a shipment as late if:

- Tracking shows the item was delivered after the estimated delivery date **unless** there is an acceptance scan within your handling time or there is confirmation from the buyer of on-time delivery.
- The buyer confirms the item was delivered after the estimated delivery date **unless** there is an acceptance scan within your handling time or there is delivery confirmation by the estimated delivery date.

Ebay's Money Back Guarantee: Buyers can have confidence when shopping on Ebay due to the site's *Money Back Guarantee.* And while this policy can frustrate sellers who may feel that a buyer is taking advantage of them, the policy is in place to ensure that all customers feel safe when shopping on Ebay so that they will return to the site again and again.

According to Ebay, "When a buyer initially starts a return because the item didn't match the listing description or reports that they didn't receive an item, the transaction issue is called a "request." If the buyer and seller can't resolve the problem, and the buyer or seller asks us to step in and help with the transaction, the request then becomes a "case."

These policies are not just public relations soundbites; they are what Ebay uses to evaluate our seller performance standards, which allow us to continue selling on their site. However, Ebay also offers many **Seller Protections**, including their **Abusive Buyer Policy**, which prohibits buyers from:

- Demanding something that was not offered in the ori-

ginal listing
- Making false claims about an order
- Misusing returns
- Misusing Ebay's messaging system or bidding platform
- Abusing the buyer protection program

Ebay also recognizes that some situations are out of both the seller's and buyer's hands; fortunately, they offer protections for events outside of a seller's control, including:

If an item arrives late, but tracking shows that you shipped it on time, Ebay will automatically adjust your late shipment rate and remove feedback as long as the carrier scan shows you shipped within your handling time; or the carrier scan shows that the item arrived by the estimated delivery, even if you shipped it late.

If there is no tracking, the order will not be counted as late as long as the buyer does not indicate that it was late. This could happen if perhaps you mailed a small, flat item via *First Class Letter* mail, or your postal carrier did not scan the shipment.

Ebay is also particularly good about protecting sellers due to severe weather or other carrier disruptions by automatically adjusting the late shipment rate, removing canceled transaction defects, and removing feedback if you are in an area identified as experiencing delivery delays if the shipment receives a carrier scan within your handling time.

Ebay updates us on their **Announcement Board** as well as on the **Ebay for Business Facebook** page whenever they identify a widespread carrier delay issue.

Messages: It is against Ebay's policies for buyers and sellers to communicate off the Ebay site regarding a transaction. All communication needs to be done through the Ebay messaging system. Not only does this provide an easy way for you to keep track of all messages from both Ebay and customers, but it protects you as a seller as there will be an online record of all communications. So, if you are ever harassed or threatened by a customer, you can easily report it to Ebay, and they will handle it.

At the **top right-hand side of your Seller Hub** page is a link for **Messages**. You will find all messages that are sent to you and where you can send messages yourself. You can modify your messaging settings under the **Change Settings** link on the top right-hand side of your *Message* page. Here you can modify your **Inbox settings, Email signature,** and **Time Away and Automatic Responses.** You can choose to **Auto archive email messages** for one, two, or three months, if at all. And there is also a section to **Set up your time away** for when you need to take a break from selling for any reason.

You need to keep communication with your buyers friendly and professional and not send messages to them needlessly. When a customer buys an item, Ebay automatically sends them a notice that they have committed to purchasing the product, and they need to pay. There is no need for you to send them a message demanding payment. I have seen so many new Ebay sellers get into trouble doing this.

Accuracy: Make sure your listing titles, item specifics, and descriptions are all accurate. Any mistakes in these areas can lead to a customer filing an **Item Not As Described** (i.e., INAD) case against you.

Non-Paying Buyers: From time to time, someone will bid on an item at auction and not pay; or, if you do not have *Immediate Payment Required* on your listings, someone may click on it but not pay. This is the nature of Ebay, so expect non-paying bidders to pop up now and again. If I have an item up for auction and it ends with a winning bidder, I log onto Ebay and send them an invoice for the order. If they do not pay by the following day, I send them a friendly note reminding them that their payment is due.

In May of 2021, Ebay updated its non-paying buyer process. Where sellers once had to actively open a case against a buyer who did not pay within four days, now Ebay allows sellers to cancel these orders automatically. Buyers still have four calendar days to pay for their items, and Ebay will automatically prompt them to pay. However, on the fifth day of not receiving payment, sellers can now cancel the sale and relist the item.

This change is a big step for dealing with non-paying buyers as Ebay used to give buyers an additional four days to pay after a case was opened. That was four days on top of the four days they initially had to pay. So, an eight-day process has now been reduced to four.

Hopefully, Ebay will eventually do the same as Poshmark, which is to automatically initiate payment from buyers when they win an auction or accept an offer from a seller. With the implementation of Managed Payments, this should be easy for Ebay to do.

Newbies: As a new seller, you may have to deal with people praying on your inexperience by sending you messages trying to get you to sell them an item for less than you have listed. If you are open to accepting offers, you need to set up the *Best Offer* option in your listing; buyers should NOT contact you to request a discount or to ask you to sell things to them off Ebay. To stay safe, keep all your transactions ON Ebay and report anyone trying to get you to deal with them offline.

Shipping: Charge fair shipping prices. While it is okay to slightly pad flat rate shipping costs to cover handling fees, keep your postal charges as close to the actual price as possible to avoid customers giving you a low rating on your shipping, i.e., "dinging your stars."

For items weighing over a pound, I advocate using *Calculated Shipping* so that buyers pay the exact shipping cost based on the weight of the item and the zip code it is going to. Ship your items the following business day (i.e., weekday). If you get a sale on a Saturday, go ahead and print the label out and prepare it for shipment Monday. Ship your items in clean packing materials. Upgrade shipping from economy (slow) to expedited (fast) when possible to exceed your buyer's expectations.

Keeping a Schedule: To sell on Ebay successfully takes a lot of WORK. Between sourcing items and listing them to answering customer questions and preparing shipments, it is easy for Ebay to take up every waking moment of your life. While attending to customers and shipping out items should always take priority, it is also essential to set realistic goals for each day so that you do not get overwhelmed.

What has worked for me is to go out "picking" (i.e., shopping at estate sales and thrift stores, often referred to these days as "sourcing") only on certain days. I take photos and only take photos on another day. On the days that I am not sourcing or taking pictures, I list. By only focusing on one area of business on a given day, I can commit to it fully and not get overwhelmed by trying to do it all in a single day. The only tasks I do every single day are answering customer questions and shipping out orders.

I also make sure to take some time off now and then. A day or two off from Ebay ensures that you do not burn out on your business. Even a few hours away from the computer to do something fun like meeting a friend for lunch or going window shopping can help you come back to Ebay with renewed energy. After all, you likely started a home-based business so that you would have more freedom and time with your family, so do not forget to take time for yourself!

If a buyer ends up not paying, and I must file a claim and then close a case, I then relist the item and block the buyer. I simply highlight and copy the buyer's Ebay screen and go to the **Blocked**

Buyers List on Ebay's site. Ebay does not make finding this page manageable, so I recommend that you do a simple internet search for "Ebay blocked bidders list" to find this page and then bookmark it for future reference.

During this entire process, the only direct contact I make with the buyer is the ONE message reminding them that their payment is due. I do not message them several times a day. I do not message them telling them I am filing a claim. And I do not message them that they have been blocked. I let Ebay handle all communication with the buyer, which they will do by sending them a message about the unpaid claim and warning them that they will get a strike if they do not submit payment.

Reporting Buyers: I always say that 99.9% of my Ebay customers are fantastic and that only .01% ever cause me problems. However, when someone is being mean or threatening online, it often feels like everyone is against you.

Fortunately, if someone is harassing you, you can report them to Ebay. Ebay is not only proactive when it comes to getting bad sellers off the site, but in recent years, they have begun to crack down harder on bad buyers, too.

Suppose someone has sent you an inappropriate message through the Ebay messaging system (trying to extort feedback or cussing at you). In that case, you can easily report them through the link provided in the **Marketplace Safety Tip** box under the message. Simply click on the **Report an inappropriate email** link. Ebay will then be able to see the message for themselves and act.

Do not engage with a threatening buyer yourself; simply ignore them and report them to Ebay. I also take the step to block them so that they cannot buy anything else from me. Again, by keeping all communication on Ebay's site, Ebay has a record of any threats or harassment, and they can act on their end, which prevents you from further dealing with problem customers.

Under-Promise & Over-Deliver: One of the best pieces of advice I got when I started selling on Ebay was to "under-promise and over-deliver." If you say you will ship items in two days, ship them in one. Print the label out as soon as you can after payment clears so that the buyer will get a notification that the item has shipped. If an item is in excellent condition, list it as "very good" so that the buyer gets more than they were expecting. Use clean packing materials and wrap items well inside their boxes to protect them during the shipping process. Upgrade shipping when possible so that customers get their orders faster than they expect.

Returns: No one who sells online likes returns. It is so exciting to sell an item and get paid, and it is a huge letdown when the customer contacts you wanting to return that item. Issuing refunds is no fun! However, accepting returns can be good practice for any business, even for someone only selling on Ebay occasionally. And when it comes to clothing, you can expect to get returns from time to time.

For years, I had my return policy set so that customers could return items they simply did not like at their own expense within 14 days. In 2019, Ebay changed the time frame to a mandatory 30 days; and they also started pushing sellers to accept "free" returns, meaning sellers had to pay the return shipping.

At that point, I opted out of returns altogether as it just was not financially feasible for me to accept returns, especially since I usually offer "free shipping" on most of my items. Paying for the shipping to AND from a customer leaves me with no room for profit when factoring in all the other fees and business expenses related to selling on Ebay.

However, if I have made a mistake when listing the item (I described the fabric wrong or took incorrect measurements), then the error is mine, and I will issue the buyer a full refund, including postage. Unless it is a high-priced item that I can easily resell, I usually just tell the customer they can keep the item to give to someone else or to donate so that I do not have to pay the return postage. If I am going to have to throw the item away myself, there is no sense paying for the buyer to ship it back to me.

If I originally paid $1 for a shirt and listed it for $15.99 with free shipping, my actual profit is only about $8 after postage and fees, including my business expense and taxes. I will not spend another $6 to have the customer return it to me so that I can relist it and only end up with a couple of dollars. Small sales like this usually are not worth the hassle of dealing with a return, and since it was my mistake, issuing a refund makes the buyer happy and lets me move on to my other sales.

Some clothing sellers do accept returns if the buyer pays the shipping, and there are a small handful of sellers who do offer "free" returns on everything they sell. What you do is up to you, but if you are just starting out selling clothing, you might find it beneficial to accept returns until you build up your feedback and get the hang of selling clothes. With Ebay's bulk editing feature, you can easily change your return policy at any time.

The best way to prevent returns or complaints is to do everything possible to accurately describe the items you are selling in the first place. Ensure you take lots of good photos, provide accurate measurements, and are honest about the item's condition. If a shirt has a tiny mark on it, disclose that in the listing AND show a picture of it. If a coat has a button missing, put that in the item condition field AND in the item description field AND take a close-up photo of it. Items with minor flaws can still sell, but to make sure the sale sticks and that the buyer does not return the item, you need to be upfront and honest in the original listing.

Buyers can get around a "no returns" policy by stating that

an item was not as described (in Ebay speak, this is called an **INAD**, i.e., **Item Not As Described**). Unfortunately, some buyers use this trick to return clothing they ended up not liking. And Ebay usually backs them up, meaning you have no choice but to not only accept the return but also to pay for the postage AND refund the buyer their total original price, including shipping. While this is highly frustrating, it happens to everyone at some point when they are selling on Ebay. I deal with this by accepting the return and relisting the item, and I also block the buyer.

When dealing with any customer issue, you want to stick to communicating only through Ebay's messaging system. If a buyer wants to make a return, they need to go through Ebay's return process, not contact you directly to arrange the return. If a buyer does contact you directly wanting to return a piece of clothing, give them these directions:

- To start a return, find the item in the Purchase history section of My eBay.
- Select the reason for the return.
- Print a return shipping label and packing slip.
- Pack the item carefully.
- You can track the status of the returned item in the Purchase history section of My eBay.

By going through Ebay's return process, both you and the buyer are protected. You can track the package and issue a refund upon the item's return to you as a seller. If you do not receive the item back and tracking proves this, Ebay will close the case and protect you from the buyer retaliating with negative feedback.

However, if you get the item back in the condition you initially shipped it, you need to log on to Ebay and close the return case. Ebay will automatically issue the buyer a refund, taking the funds from your *Pending Balance* account. At that point, you can just relist the item. Clothing that is returned and then relisted has a higher sell-thru rate as Ebay's algorithm favors listings with a sales history, so sometimes returned items sell almost immediately after you relist them.

So, what is the best way to keep your account in good standing, even when dealing with unexpected emergencies or demanding customers? Here are my tips:

1. Make sure your listings are accurate with the correct measurements, conditions, and item specifics. Also, provide lots of clear photos showing the item from every angle so that customers know exactly what they are buying.
2. Do not steal other seller's photos or use stock photos unless you have permission from the company.
3. Make sure you meet your handling time. My handling time is two business days, but I almost always ship the next business day. However, the extra day acts as a buffer in case something comes up.
4. Upgrade shipping when possible. Be sure to check all the shipping options available when you go to print your postage. You may find that you can provide an expedited shipping service for the exact cost as the economy option.
5. Respond to customer questions promptly and professionally.
6. Package your items well to prevent breakage.
7. If you get a return request or a message from a buyer saying the item arrived damaged, take a deep breath, and direct them on how to use Ebay's return system to file a claim. Do not get into a fight via messaging; Ebay's system is set up to handle claims and returns.
8. If Ebay sides in a buyer's favor, it is okay to be upset but do not let it ruin your day or your business. See if you could have done anything differently to affect the outcome and implement those lessons as you con-

tinue selling.
9. Do not use the Ebay messaging system for anything other than talking to Ebay customers about specific listings. Do not offer to sell something off the Ebay site. Do not give buyers your phone number or email address. Do not reply to harassing messages, either; report those immediately to Ebay and let them handle it.
10. Over-promise and over-deliver!

The following are some of the most common questions I have gotten over the years in regards to problems on Ebay:

HELP! A customer wants me to end an auction early and sell an item to them for a set price! When you place an item up for auction, you may have someone message you that they will buy the item if you end the auction.

Bottom line: Do NOT do this! People like this are likely trying to low-ball you because they think they can get the item for less than it will go for at auction. When I get messages like this, I reply that the auction is already in motion with watchers and will not end it early. Period!

HELP! A customer claims they have not received their package, yet tracking shows it was delivered! This comes up every so often, and it is usually a case where someone else in the home has taken in the package, or it was delivered to a neighbor. I ask the customer to double-check, reminding them that tracking shows their order was delivered.

Once they know you have tracking (which is why you should always ship through Ebay), you would be amazed how quickly buyers find their missing packages! Sadly, there are people out there who try to get full refunds on their orders by saying they have not arrived. But as long as you have shipped your packages through Ebay and have a valid tracking number, Ebay will back the transaction up in your favor.

HELP! A customer says their item arrived broken! When a customer messages me that their item arrived broken, I calmly reply that I am so sorry and ask them to provide me with a photo of the damage. Do NOT just blindly give out refunds; it is important to ask for proof. Ebay has added the ability to attach photos in their messaging system, so it is easy for buyers to send you a picture.

There are scammers out there who break their own item, buy a replacement on Ebay, and then try to pass off their original broken item like the one they just bought. While these scams are very rare, they do happen.

If you get a picture of an item that is broken, you will have to issue a refund. If you do not, the customer will file a claim with Ebay, and Ebay will automatically refund their money by taking it out of your pending balance. While this can be frustrating, it is just a part of selling online. And it will make you want to ensure that your orders are packaged to the best of your ability. If you are shipping the package through USPS Priority Mail, it is automatically insured for up to $50, so you can file a claim with the Post Office to recoup your loss.

HELP! I got an email from Ebay saying I need to reset my account OR that my account has been suspended or that I need to verify my identity and click on a link in the email! Remember that ALL Ebay messages go through Ebay's messaging system; you will NEVER get an email from Ebay or PayPal sent directly to your email address without a copy of it also being in your Ebay messages. Any email asking for your password or for you to click on a link to take a survey is a SCAM. Ignore it and delete it! Only respond to Ebay messages WITHIN your Ebay messaging system WITHIN your Ebay account!

HELP! My item isn't selling! Did your item have any watchers? Did anyone ask you questions about it? Take a good look at your listing to see if you can improve on it by writing a better title, including more photos, or adding to the description. Maybe your price was too high, or you had it at *Auction* when it would sell better at *Fixed Price*. Edit your listing and then relist it with the changes. If it does not sell the second time around and it is not getting any traffic or watchers, it may be better to pull it to donate or sell at your own garage sale.

HELP! A customer is threatening to leave me negative feedback if I don't do something, and/or they are cursing at me! Feedback extortion is NOT allowed on Ebay; neither is foul nor threatening language. Report messages like this immediately!

To Recap: Even if you follow all the tips and tricks in this book designed to avoid most customer problems, you will inevitably occasionally run into issues when selling on Ebay. Fortunately, Ebay provides several safeguards to protect both buyers and sellers. You want to resolve all issues through Ebay's messaging and reporting systems; do not attempt to problem solve through direct email or by phone. Doing so will void any seller's protection you may be eligible for.

In business, the customer is always right (even when you know they are wrong!), so it is essential to have a good set of customer policies in place so that both you and the buyer understand what is expected of one another. Ebay, of course, has its own set of policies that you must adhere to, such as giving buyers two business days to pay for their items. You cannot demand someone pay you within an hour as that is not Ebay's rule. When you sell on Ebay, you must first follow Ebay's rules. Ebay is not YOUR business; it is a TOOL you use in your business. Use the tools they provide to make your Ebay journey a success!

CONCLUSION

Whether you picked up this book because you wanted to start selling on Ebay or because you wanted to take your Ebay business to the next level, I hope you found the information helpful!

I have been selling on Ebay since 2005, and I have had to pivot my business model more times than I can count. Ebay and the online selling landscape are constantly changing and evolving, hence why I publish new editions of this book every year. But regardless of how retail has changed over the years, one thing remains the same: Ebay is still in the top three of online shopping sites. Whatever you have to sell, you will have the best chance of selling it on Ebay.

From sourcing and photographing to listing and shipping, selling on Ebay takes work. But the rewards can be well worth the time and effort you put into it. Whether you are just looking to earn a bit of extra spending money or want to start your own home-based business, Ebay offers sellers of every size the opportunity to earn an income.

The only thing standing in the way of you making money on Ebay is YOU! The more you list, the more you will sell. So, get to listing and watch the money roll in!

ABOUT THE AUTHOR

Ann Eckhart is a writer, reseller, and online content creator based in Iowa. She has numerous books available about how to make money online and from home. Check out her Amazon Author Page at https://amzn.to/34nE9us for all her titles.

You can also follow Ann Eckhart on these social media sites:

FACEBOOK: https://www.facebook.com/anneckhart/

TWITTER: https://twitter.com/ann_eckhart

INSTAGRAM: https://www.instagram.com/ann_eckhart/

YOUTUBE CHANNEL: https://tinyurl.com/yxvqtwc7

COPYRIGHT 2021

Made in the USA
Middletown, DE
21 August 2022